EUROPEAN UNION:
FORTRESS OR DEMOCRACY?

EUROPEAN UNION: FORTRESS OR DEMOCRACY?

Towards a Democratic Market and a New Economic Order

MICHAEL BARRATT BROWN

SPOKESMAN
for
EUROPEAN LABOUR FORUM

First published in Great Britain in 1991 by
Spokesman
Bertrand Russell House
Gamble Street
Nottingham, England
Tel. 0602 708318

British Library Cataloguing in Publication Data

Barratt Brown, Michael 1918 — European union:
fortress or democracy?
1. Economic development. Political aspects
I. Title
330.9

ISBN 0-85124-520-X
ISBN 0-85124-521-8 pbk

Printed by the Russell Press Ltd, Nottingham
(Tel.0602 784505)

CONTENTS

Introduction

1991 will be remembered as the year of the Gulf War. But after it 1992 is not only the year when the European Community becomes a single market, with all the economic implications for associated countries as well as for the twelve members; it will be the crunch year for Eastern Europe's transition to a market economy, and perhaps most important of all the year when bridges will have to be built from Europe to the peoples of the Third World of developing countries, whose hearts and minds were never won for a military settlement of the Gulf crisis. This book is inspired by the fear that preoccupation with purely European questions will lead to neglect of Europe's responsibility for the desparate situation in the Third World countries, which are almost without exception one-time European colonies.

This book is addressed particularly to those who like myself were opposed to Britain's entry into the Common Market in 1975 or have remained scared, if not antagonistic, as the European Commission has spread the tentacles of its regulations over the body politic of one-time sovereign nation states. The key issue has always been that of democratic control — what democratric powers were able to offset the bureaucratic powers of the Commission and what popular forces could be mobilised to compensate for the unequal strength of people and institutions in a common market.

For many of us, the nation state and the power of national associations, and particularly of organised labour, offered the only realisable countervailing power. In this book it is argued that such national resources are no longer adequate. In face of the concentrated power of the combinations of capital in the giant European companies, nothing less will do but that European-wide structures — both political and economic — should be built and maintained and European-wide social policies should be conceived and fought for.

The European Parliament is already in place, but with quite inadequate powers of democratic control over the Commission. A European Trade Union Confederation exists, but with no collective bargaining powers to negotiate with European capital. The British Trade Union Congress and some national unions have proposed policies for resisting the worst effects of a single market, but no common set of policies has been put forward apart from the Commission's own outline draft for a Social Charter.

Socialism as an economic system has become discredited because of its association in the East with authoritarian command structures of planning. These have proved to be effective in waging war and in post-war reconstruction, but have failed to harness human energies for meeting the needs of peacetime life, or to exploit natural resources without prodigious waste and damage to the environment. The market as the main world economic organising system is looked to for salvation. But, while the market has enabled the majority of the population in the North to increase enormously the quantity and range of their consumption, the minority has benefited little, and in the much larger populations of the South it is only the minority that has gained. Nothing less than constant government regulation of the market has checked the tendency for inequalities to grow, and market regulation has done no better than centralised commands in protecting the environment and conserving scarce resources. In the event, rising debts and falling incomes have led to internecine struggle and military adventure.

Faced with this dilemma, politicians and economists have begun to talk about the "social market", of "market socialism", and of ways to combine planning and the market. For such talk to become more than playing with words, it is necessary that some content should be given to the several concepts and their relationship to each other. What structures of plan and market can realistically be combined? What social regulation can the market take without destroying its capacity to encourage enterprise and initiative? What market freedoms can be permitted without endangering the egalitarian aims of socialism? What is the proper balance between social provision and individual appropriation? The answers to these questions cannot be determined in some absolute sense. They will depend on the purpose that is intended. Both markets and plans can be regulated in an authoritarian way or in a democratic way. The purpose intended in this book is the widest possible distribution of power and wealth.

The argument advanced here is that new European-wide political and economic structures must take account of new forms of popular association, and new means of instantaneous cross-frontier communication. The environmental crisis has spawned a plethora of "green" organisations. Rejection of fast, mass-produced food has generated a host of alternative trade shops. Centralised state power has produced a centrifugal burgeoning of ethnic minorities and ancient regional loyalties, with horizontal linkages across frontiers. At the same time, personal computers, electronic mail and fax machines have put into the hands of the smallest groups the means of communication and co-ordination of activities which were until recently the prerogative of only the largest corporations and state organisations.

In these circumstances new European-wide policies cannot just be a cobbling together of existing state practices, which have imposed a modicum of planning and regulation on the free working of the market. The dichotomy of plan and market, public and private, economy and polity has been transformed into the co-operative networking of competing enterprises which are challenging both big business methods and state bureaucracy with the weapons of flexible automation and new information technology.

None of this carries with it any necessary advantage for democracy; rather the opposite. The technology has been developed by the giant transnational companies, for their own purposes and under their own control. But it can be used also for extending democratic controls, for widening and deepening the power that ordinary men and women have over their own lives. To have this result, not only new structures linking producers and consumers in new ways have to be created, but new ideas are needed in our thinking about economic growth and development.

What follows is designed to generate discussion of the problems and possible solutions. The *European Labour Forum*, sponsored by the Socialist Group of the European Parliament, has begun the process of opening up discussion. It is hoped that the papers in this book will continue that process in somewhat greater depth.

Some of the following chapters were written in connection with my work with Third World Information Network (TWIN). They have been discussed with my colleagues in TWIN and could not have been attempted without the experience which TWIN has had in working on development problems with partners from the South and also from the East. Many of the ideas in the papers come from both colleagues and partners, but they are not to be held responsible for the way in which I have interpreted our experience. I am also grateful to Regan Scott for most helpful comments on an earlier draft of the first chapter.

At the same time, I have also benefited greatly, as always, from discussion of earlier drafts of the papers with my friend and colleague in the Bertrand Russell Peace Foundation, Ken Coates. His experience in the Socialist Group in the European Parliament has encouraged me to believe that there is now a real possibility that ideas for a new economic order might still be listened to. If this book contributes, in however small a way, to the discussion of alternative forms of economic development and international trade, that will be reward enough.

Inevitably in such a short compass many of the arguments and proposals are presented without adequate substantiation and without references to the work of others on whom I have relied. A fuller exposition can be found in two forthcoming books: *A Piece of the Action: Fair Trading with the Third World* and *A Future for Socialism in Europe.*

Michael Barratt Brown
February 1991

CHAPTER 1

Into Europe: All or Nothing

An underview

This review of the prospects for Europe after 1992 is deliberately called an "underview", and not an "overview", because what is happening in the European Community is too often seen from above, from the position of the European Commission, of the several governments and the European Parliament. Too little attention is given to the role of the European peoples, the men and women of the twelve states and their several different national communities. Yet the power of ordinary people in the streets was shown most vividly in the change of political direction in Eastern Europe in 1989 and it is, ironically, among some of the minority nationalities — Scots and Irish, Breton and Basque, Sicilian and Catalan — that most interest is evinced in the progressive access of power by the European Community's institutions.

Joining the European Community in the 1970s was presented to the British people as a great opportunity for British industry, so long in decline, to share in wider markets, and for British culture, so long diverted into overseas empire, to be reunited with its European roots. The two "English diseases" of industrial conservatism and of political isolationism would be cured at a stroke. Many of us warned that competition could kill as well as cure, and that a true internationalism could not be limited to the West End of Europe. The most obvious central location for investment in Western Europe was around the mouth of the Rhine. Britain was inevitably on the periphery. The alternative of building on Commonwealth links to establish new and fairer world-wide international economic relations was derided on the Left as neo-colonialist and on the Right as utopian dreaming.

What actually happened after the 1975 referendum had confirmed Britain's entry into the European Community was neither what the Common Market enthusiasts had promised nor quite what we had warned. The British economy went through a disastrous process of de-Industrialisation, as imports of manufactures, partly from Europe, partly from Japan, replaced domestic production. These imports were paid for from the bonanza of North Sea oil, which also made possible massive capital investments overseas, the capital flowing mainly to the USA, both in portfolio and direct investment. Whereas in the 1960s and 1970s about a quarter of all British capital investment went abroad and three-quarters stayed at home, the proportions rose in the 1980s to half abroad and half at home, the same as in the great period of Britain's overseas investment in the nineteenth and early twentieth centuries. Only a part of this recent capital outflow was offset by capital inflows, mainly for North Sea oil development.

As imports of manufactured goods have steadily replaced home-made products, it has happened that for the first time in two hundred years the value of manufactured goods imported into Britain is greater than the value exported. The penetration of foreign manufactures in sectors of industry like office machinery and data processing is almost total, while the proportion of imports in relation to home demand exceeds 50% in motor transport, instrument and electrical engineering, clothing and footwear. The switch from home to overseas investment has had the effect not only of reducing industrial employment at home but also of redistributing incomes. When capital is invested in activities overseas rather than at home, the result is that investment which directly creates jobs at home is replaced by investment which brings income to the investors. This only indirectly creates jobs at home in providing services for the investors, together with luxury goods like yachts, jewelry, *haut couture*, five star hotels and smart restaurants.

Britain has become increasingly a service economy. Employment in industry has been steadily replaced by employment in services, but to say this conceals a major switch in jobs from full-time employment to part-time, with a huge increase in part-time jobs for women, and from jobs in the old industrial areas of Central London and the North to jobs in the new towns and distribution points and recreational areas of the South. This has generated unequal development — the growth of rentier incomes mainly in the South, dependent on overseas investment, while dereliction and poverty have been the lot of the North. The result in the last ten years is that the top tenth of the population have doubled their real incomes, but the bottom tenth have actually grown poorer.

This polarising of wealth and poverty in Britain has been aggravated by the Thatcher Government's tax concessions to the rich and cuts in social provision for the poor, bearing particularly hard upon the increased numbers of pensioners and unemployed. While on the continent public expenditure, especially on health and education and the basic infrastructure of railways, roads, water and sewerage, has been stepped up, in Britain it has been cut back. Far from general social living standards rising in line throughout Europe, Britain has fallen back to a level where only Eire, Portugal and Greece stand lower in the league table. In many matters of welfare, especially for women — equal pay for equal work, children's allowances, maternity leave, paid holidays and insurance for part-time as well as full-time workers, — most other countries are far ahead of Britain in their provision. As for the anticipated mutual enrichment of cultures, the opening up of travel has meant fish and chips and punch-ups in Benidorm, and hooliganism by British fans before and after football matches on the continent.

What should Britain do now?

After fifteen years of full membership of the European Community and a resultant total shift in British trade — from a quarter of our trade conducted with the European Common Market to well over a half — there is no possibility now of withdrawing. Our old trading partners in the Commonwealth have gone elsewhere or fallen back from lack of development. The only two options are either the half-way house of an economic community of sovereign states, or full federation in a United States of Europe. When those of us who once argued against Britain's entry into the Community at any price now recommend full federation, we have some explaining to do. The fact is that the half-way house is not a true option; it is a political ploy, pretending to some special relationship of Britain with the USA, and winning the votes of those who hark back to some period of imperial greatness. The sovereignty of a nation state today, except perhaps for the super powers (if there are still two), is so much limited by the internationalisation of capital in giant transnational companies that it is an illusion to imagine that the British government can fix British interest rates or the rate of exchange of the pound with other currencies. These rates are determined by the competitive movements of goods and capital among the giant companies, for whom national barriers are largely an irrelevance. Or, where they are not irrelevant, they are an opportunity for the giant companies to divide and conquer, in obtaining concessions on taxes, labour relations and environmental controls for locating their investment in one nation state rather than in another.

Fifteen years ago the trend towards world economic domination by giant companies was already clear, although the process of merger and take-over among the giants themselves has since then greatly speeded up. Why was there an alternative then that does not exist now? The alternative internationalist approach at that time was only in part a matter of creating a non-aligned bloc of Scandinavian and Commonwealth countries which could stand up to the super powers, or to the Europe of the original Six, or to the rising power of Japan. It was much more to use the strength of such a non-aligned bloc that embraced both Northern First World and Southern Third World countries to press for the revival of the United Nations' political and economic authority, in place of the dual hegemony of the super powers. Now that one of these powers, starting from a lower economic base and having suffered devastation in two world wars, has been defeated in a fiercely accelerating arms race, where do we stand? The United States government is once again reclaiming its erstwhile sole hegemony, but its economic power is under challenge from both Japan and Germany, who are in fact supplying the finance for the vast United States trade deficit.

The argument for strengthening the structure of the European Community is not only to have a framework to contain German ambitions, but also once again to have a base from which to press for restoring the authority of the United Nations. While the United States held an unquestioned world hegemony, the United Nations was bound to be diminished. Today, with major centres of power in Japan and Western Europe, and potentially in the Soviet Union and China, challenging the USA, a new international order is on the agenda. The crisis in the Persian Gulf has revealed the importance of ensuring that the authority of the United Nations is asserted in matters of life and death for the whole human race. And it is of much significance that the European Community, both the Commission and the Parliament, are keeping their distance from the military involvement in the Middle East of the United States dogs of war and their British poodle. But just to reveal the division between Britain and the other European Community members over this issue raises the question most sharply of the choice between a loose confederation for Europe, which Mrs. Thatcher long advocated, and full federation, to which most of the other Community members, and apparently the Labour Party, are committed. The prospect of adding to the Community not just East Germany, but the rest of Eastern Europe, and probably Austria, and who else — the Baltic states and Scandinavia? — greatly complicates the answer that has to be given sooner or later. The motivation of the several states now outside the Community for joining a single Europe is a dual one — military security and economic viability. The two are separate but related. They are equally important for making a judgement about Britain's stance.

The disappearance of the *raison d'être* for Nato has evidently not resulted in any desire among members to dissolve the alliance. The Gulf conflict has been greeted as a reason for continuing it. But without the Warsaw Pact, there is a need and the possibility for an all-European security system to ensure the peaceful settlement of disputes. The CSCE (Conference on Security and Co-operation in Europe), which brings together all European states, including the USSR, with the USA and Canada, has been proposed for this role; and Frank Blackaby has suggested how this might work, especially in the disarmament processes where it already has experience. It would need to have a permanent location and secretariat and a structure of inner and outer members, if it were to become an effective peace-keeping body; and it would have to be brought under the aegis of the United Nations as a regional agency, if it were to have international authority, and it would need then to be related to the United Nations' economic functions, as well as to its peace-making role. There would then be a need also for the discussions on the reduction of Conventional Forces in Europe (CFE) to be linked to UN authorisation.

Three awkward problems remain even within a new European security system — the relations between a wider European Community and a possibly disintegrating Soviet Union; the difficulty of a new United States of Europe simply taking over the seats of France and the UK on the UN Security Council (although it would solve the problem of Germany's continued absence, which is a standing source of weakness in the authority of the UN); and the future of the close military integration of the USA and Western Europe in armaments manufacture and control, especially in the case of nuclear weapons, and in army command structures. The last problem may be expected to wither away as more and more states follow France and Spain in withholding their armed forces from Nato command, and as Japanese and German technology increasingly predominate, although this will not happen without much resistance from US manufacturers. The other problems may be even more intractable.

To some whose voices cannot be ignored, both on the Left (Tony Benn) and on the Right of British politics (John Biffen), isolation of the Soviet Union from an otherwise united Europe and abrogation of British sovereignty, above all in her place on the Security Council, are reasons enough for supporting a loose confederation and not a Federal Europe. But this is not a choice which is available. There is no possibility of the eleven members of the Community giving up their progress towards a federal Europe. The question is whether the UK joins in with them, and how many others from the East and

North are to be incorporated. There are at least three or four possible Europes: the eleven including East Germany and probably Austria; the rest of Eastern Europe; the rich northern EFTA (European Free Trade Association) members, including perhaps the UK; and then there is the Soviet Union. To have the eleven develop into federal union, and leave the East outside, is really to encourage a fortress mentality inside, and to create turmoil and ruin outside — starving masses burdened by debt and fighting to get in. The Berlin wall was nothing to the wall building that will be in order again, from the Oder right down to the Adriatic.

Bringing the eastern European states into a wider federation appears to be the only way to ensure that the debts are written off or scaled down, and resources are transferred from the rich half of Europe to the poor half, so as to prevent the collapse of employment and food supplies and total breakdown of law and order in the East. If the EFTA countries are included at the same time, the resources available will be that much greater. Inevitably, such a transfer must imply some reduction in the living standards of the rich, at least for a period of time. But the economy, like peace, is indivisible. A narrow fortress offers a restricted market; defending the wall will not be costless, and who would choose to live on an island of affluence in a sea of misery?

At the same time, those who would hold Britain back from joining in the march towards federation have to recognise what would be the result inside the fortress. This would leave Germany, after re-incorporating East Germany and possibly Austria, without any restraining framework in the matter of economic power, even if a greatly strengthened CSCE takes care of the security question. Would this be enough to give new authority to the United Nations, and if Germany were added to the members of the Security Council would that be enough to contain a possible revival of German ambitions? Would a wider federal Europe serve better, or might it become itself a greater Germany? The answer to these questions must depend on the nature of the federal structure and of the policies pursued within it.

A wider Europe?
It is hardly possible to imagine the inclusion of the Soviet Union, with its vast Asian territories and populations, inside an all-European Federation, although the Socialist project once envisaged all the European peoples coming within a Union of Socialist Soviet Republics. Relations between a 400 million United States of Europe and a 300 million USSR remain the most difficult to prescribe. We simply do not know enough about the way the peoples of the USSR

regard their continued membership of the Union. All sorts of irridentist movements have emerged from the Baltic to the Caspian Sea. But Gorbachev's appeal to a sense of realism about access to oil and electric power seems to be working, with the help of some show of force, and could hold the Union together, if food and consumer goods production and distribution can be re-established.

Nor do we know enough about the eastern European peoples' wishes. Having just emerged from decades of Soviet rule, they are in no mood to continue the association, even if the conditions were changed. We have to take into account also the long history of suspicion of Russian power in Scandinavia and in Central Europe. There are no easy answers to the problem of finding a new way of living together in peace for what have been, for so many centuries, Western and Eastern European Empires. For this reason it seems best to find a framework for a process of exploring the possibilities of developing a new relationship together among representatives of the peoples involved.

A beginning of such a process has been suggested in a proposal for a joint meeting of the European Parliament and the Supreme Soviet. This proposal, which was initiated by Ken Coates, MEP, seems likely to be accepted on both sides. Such a meeting could be prepared for and followed up by meetings of the several committees of the two Parliaments, to explore all the many aspects of a new relationship. These will include not only structures for political and economic co-operation, but all the practical matters of improved trade and transport and communication, and above all of action to protect the environment, including the rivers and forests and seas, which are the common heritage of all Europeans.

None of these suggestions for settling European problems can be considered outside of the context of world-wide relationships. Europe has for so many centuries been the cauldron of war, and European rivalries the occasion for violent conquest and colonial rule over non-European peoples. Now, the withdrawal of this rule has left many fires burning outside Europe. It is perfectly understood among peoples outside of Europe and North America that it has been the struggle for supremacy between two groups of European people that lined up allies for either side throughout the whole world and nearly brought the planet to destruction in nuclear war. In working for peaceful solutions to the many problems left behind from these conquests and divisions, much will depend on finding a permanent solution to Europe's discords, which the new realism in the Soviet leadership has made possible. But as much will depend on the progress made in rebuilding the world-wide economic order, to replace the structures erected at Bretton Woods in 1944 around the then hegemonic position of the United States.

Some of the problems of creating a new world economic order are discussed later in this book, especially as concerns the relations of a wider Europe with the Third World. Here it needs only to be said that two key elements which were then neutered, might well be revitalised. These were, first, the International Trade Organisation (ITO), which was reduced from a positive trade development agency to the monitoring role of the General Agreement on Tariffs and Trade (GATT), and , second, the UN regional Economic Commissions that lost their reconstruction powers to make way for the Marshall Plan, and became little more than research and conference centres. The UN Economic Commission for Europe, which under Gunnar Myrdal as director general immediately after 1946 had a high profile, has two great advantages for building bridges between a wider Europe and the rest of the world. It comprises all the European states including the Soviet Union and could in the economic sphere combine with the CSCE in the military sphere to relate all-European policy making to that in the Soviet Union. At the same time, it is structurally linked through all the other UN regional Economic Commissions, and also through the specialist agencies of the UN — FAO, UNESCO, WHO, etc. — to the Third World. Trade development for smaller companies in Europe — East and West — and in the Third World, effected through an ITO and through the regional commissions of the UN, could provide a crucial counterweight to the massed powers of European transnational companies, including those based in West Germany.

We have been talking about the development of a "wider Europe" as if this was an inevitable outcome of the collapse of the East European economies and the magnetic attraction of an increasingly wealthy Western Europe. But in fact the argument at the highest levels, around the President of the European Commission, is against any widening beyond the present twelve. It was Mrs. Thatcher who saw merit in widening out to embrace others. The explanation is obvious: M. Delors wishes to see the firm establishment of the single market in 1992, with European Economic and Monetary Union in place soon after, before bringing others into the fold. Mrs. Thatcher, although forced by her own failing economy to accept the Exchange Rate Mechanism (ERM), wished to stop its evolution into Economic and Monetary Union (EMU), since this must be the next step towards federation. For her, all additions to the present twelve made EMU more difficult to achieve. Adding new members to an existing EMU would be much easier, as both she and M. Delors knew full well.

Mrs. Thatcher's anxiety to resist all development towards a federal Europe derived from her belief in the sovereignty of nation states. Apart from the rhetoric that surrounds the appeal to national sovereignty, the exercise of sovereignty looks quite different to those whose view comes from above, from representing the nation at international conferences, or commanding the nations armed forces in the field, and to those who look from below, at the decisions that are handed down and at what it means to serve the nation and lay down one's own life for the sovereign. *Dulce et decorum est pro patria mori* is not a claim that has many takers today. Taking an underview does not suggest any obvious reasons for preserving a power structure which has grown up around the fabled exploits of heroic national figures in the past. We shall take a long, hard look at the real advantages to be derived from a separate currency and national budgets when we look in later chapters at the implications of a common currency and federal budgets.

Given the possibility, even probability, of the European Community moving towards a federal structure, are there strong reasons to be adduced against a widening of the European Community to encompass all of Europe, only excluding the Soviet Union? To the present 300 million population another 100 to 150 million would be added. These seem big numbers compared with the United States' 250 million and the Soviet Union's 280 million, but they are easily dwarfed by India's 800 million, or China's 1200 million. Large states with federal structures may allow more autonomy for minority nations than do unitary states. The size of a federal Europe will depend upon the number of nations that wish to federate, once the parameters of a security system and of economic co-operation have been established. If divisions of East and West no longer have any ideological meaning in terms of the "two systems", nor should adherence to the dogmatic interpretation of the "free market", which Mrs. Thatcher was preaching during her visits to Eastern Europe. The details of democratic and federal structures must all be negotiable. Those who find themselves able to agree to work together will join; those who can't will stay outside.

The meaning of 1992
What, then, are we to say about the choice that men and women in Britain will have to make in response to the options which our political leaders are offering to us for our future in Europe? Much of the argument about these options, which is engaged in the chapters which follow, concerns the way in which both markets and plans have to be regulated in order to correct the tendency of

both to perpetuate and to aggravate inequalities. This could be seen in the planned economies of the East, but it is even more evident in the market economies of the West. The thesis of this book is that the nation state can no longer correct these tendencies, nor could a confederation of nation states, but a federation just might. A federal structure is not a sufficient condition for redistributing wealth from rich to poor, whether persons, groups or regions; that we can see from the gross and increasing inequalities in the United States of America. But it could still be a necessary condition. Let us consider, then, the implications of the first step towards federation which the single market will involve after 1992. Taking as our test case the position of the British people, what will be needed to make this step a beneficial one for them?

Entry into the Common Market meant the elimination of all tariff barriers to the movement of goods, and of all controls over the movement of capital. What does the single market, to be established in 1992, add to that? After this year, all the remaining barriers to free competition inside the Community in respect of goods and services, labour and capital, land ownership and professional qualifications will disappear. Britain will join the other states in an Economic and Monetary Union which will move towards a common currency — the ECU — and common monetary policies. The protection which is widely granted to domestic contractors in central and local government purchasing will no longer be permitted. Restrictions on work permits will be outlawed. Industrial relations, health and safety requirements, technical specifications, and transport regulations will all have to be be standardised, and professional qualifications universally recognised.

What is the likely effect on British industry of such an opening up of competition? One way of judging is to compare levels of productivity and the advantages of larger scale production, industry by industry. I have done this in a pamphlet entitled *Europe 1992*, published by the European Labour Forum. Only in a few industries — metals, chemicals, pharmaceuticals, artificial fibres, tobacco, drink, food and textiles — does British industry have levels of output per person more than half those of United States or German industry; and only in pharmaceuticals and chemicals will there be much advantage to be gained from the wider market. In the most modern industries of electronics and instruments, aircraft, motor cars, machine tools and electrical goods the levels of productivity in British industry are less than a quarter of those in the USA; and the advantages in the wider market for more productive firms are very great. The prospects for employment are grim for workers in British industry, and the possibility of emigrating to West Germany, where the investment in modern industry is massive, has been pre-empted by the flood of workers from East Germany.

With the lowest wages in the Community except for Greece, Portugal and Eire, there should be an attraction for capital to be invested in Britain when all the barriers are down. What makes Britain unattractive to investors is the poor quality of management and the low level of education of the workers. Sir Claus Moser has recently been spelling out the inadequacies of British education — class-ridden, inflexible, narrow, undemanding and inferior in quality and duration compared with that existing in all the other developed industrial countries. A motor car worker in Germany or Japan, at every level from the shop floor to top management, will have had three times the length of education after the age of fifteen of his opposite number in the British motor car industry. Is it possible that this time the effect of exposure to such competition will be to cure and not to kill? The answer to that question lies, I believe, with that much maligned and neglected species of men and women — the British trade unionist.

The role of the unions after 1992

A lie which is repeated often enough comes to be believed. One such lie is the assertion that the decline of British industry throughout this century, and most particularly in the last fifty years, is the result of the over-reaching power of the trade unions in Britain. The truth is almost certainly that, far from being too strong, they have generally been too weak to be effective. Deeply divided in their separate crafts and trades, between skilled and unskilled, they were ever more concerned with negative defensive actions to preserve their restrictive practices and wage differentials than to present a positive united challenge to management to invest profits in new plant and so raise productivity and the general level of earnings. The strength of the German unions both before the First World War and since the Second is often decried in British trade union circles because *mitbestimmung* and factory councils are regarded as incorporating workers too much into management, so that their independent organisations are undermined. The higher wages and better conditions that resulted from the increased productivity cannot be denied. There is today a real possibility that the low wage levels in Britain, and also in East Germany, could be used by employers in West Germany and elsewhere in Europe to reverse the gains made in the past by the German unions.

The obvious danger for workers inherent in the single market after 1992 is that employee rights and welfare services should be levelled downwards to the lowest standards rather than upwards to the highest. In almost every aspect of employment rights and welfare provision conditions are better across the channel than they are in Britain. We have already noted many of the benefits available especially to women workers, including those working part-time. We need to add the right to strike and to take secondary action in support of a strike, and to note that in many countries there is a minimum wage both for adults and young persons. Jacques Delors, the President of the European Commission, was so concerned in 1988 that there would be no adequate countervailing force to oppose the strength of the giant European companies when the single market opened in 1992, and the whole process would be discredited, that he attended the annual Trade Union Congress in Britain to call for British unions to join the "social dialogue". By this he meant cross border discussions between trade unions and employers' organisations to build a platform of social rights based on a European Social Charter. Without this, what has come to be called "social dumping" would be inevitable, with a general levelling down to the worst practices of each country. If working people are to strengthen their position in relation to the giant companies after 1992, there is no doubt that they will have to look to their unions.

A major advantage in moving towards a common European currency would be that workers in different countries would be able to recognise at once not only the relative values of their wages, but the relative values of all the different types of social provision in the several European Community member countries. It is immediately clear in a shop what are the relative prices of cars, or washing machines, or TV sets, or videos coming from different countries. But the payment of so many francs a week in children 's allowances or maternity leave in France, or of old age pensions at half of the average wage of so many Deutschmarks in Germany, has no meaning for British workers, unless it can be measured in relation to the purchasing power of British wages.

A common monetary policy has to be complemented by a common fiscal policy. Monetary union supplies a common discipline against inflationary tendencies, and a common framework for balancing trade with the outside world. But it does nothing to correct the tendency for uneven development in different regions of the Community. Indeed, without fiscal regulation to redistribute incomes, monetary union could make for worsening inequalities. This is because the representatives of the most advanced industrial regions, and especially from West Germany, would have the greatest influence, and would choose monetary policies which erred on the side of budgetary caution. This leads to cuts in regional and local spending where the tax base is weak, and leaves no room for expansionary measures to revive areas of declining activity — and Britain is bound to have several of these. In the Basic Document of the European Commission on Economic and Monetary Union, adopted in August 1990, there is an absolute insistence on "sound financial measures" and opposition to budget deficits that are "excessively high". Other negative warnings are only partially offset by concern at regional disparities which might need special financial support schemes.

It has been the central economic role of the nation state in the past to protect employment within its own boundaries by a mixture of fiscal and monetary measures, although the Thatcher Government did less than most in this respect. And some have claimed that we need to retain our national sovereignty for government to continue to perform this role. There was a certain irony in Mrs Thatcher's claim that she would not give up British sovereignty in these matters, seeing how little she had exercised it. But she was honest enough to make the point that it was the social regulation over the market, which she has been busy dismantling from London, that she did not wish to see re-established from Brussels. She claimed that it was the value of the pound sterling which she was protecting under British sovereignty. In making this claim, she was deceiving us and maybe was herself deceived. The last ten years have shown that a policy whose main aim was to preserve the value of the pound from inflation left us with a pound that bought less than half of what it did in 1979, and was two-thirds of the value of the ECU which it held at that time. And this despite the absence, until the Gulf crisis, of rising oil prices, and indeed the enjoyment by the Thatcher Governments of a North Sea oil bonanza, which should have held up the value of the pound. The fact is that today one nation state, even a relatively large and advanced industrial state like Britain, cannot protect its currency, or manage its exchange rate or interest rate on its own.

The importance of trade union pressure behind a campaign for fiscal measures to support a Social Charter in the European Community is clearly revealed by the signal success of the pressure group which has so far hogged the European budget — the farmers of Europe. The Common Agricultural Policy with its array of farm support systems, stockpiles and levies at present absorbs two-thirds of the whole Community budget. This will have to be modified and complemented by much greater expenditure on disadvantaged regions and localities, if these are to be saved from decay, while overcrowding and overdevelopment take place in a few geographically favoured locations. There are powerful conservationist and environmental arguments, as well as arguments on grounds of equity, to support such expenditure from a common European budget. There is no doubt that the European Commission and the European Parliament are well aware of these arguments, but the reluctance of member states, and particularly of the British, to relinquish the control of public spending to common European institutions has so far held back adequate levels of Community expenditure, with the single exception of the farm budget.

There is a little more to it than just concern for national sovereignty. Coal and steel producing communities have comprised the one other group besides the farming communities which have received large scale support from the Community budget. In both cases, this support for regions of economic decline was part of the bargain on which the European institutions were founded — the Coal and Steel Community under the Treaty of Paris, and then the Economic Community under the Treaty of Rome — and incorporated into the Treaties' articles. On this analogy, the bargain which Britain should claim for opening up British markets in 1992 and entering the EMU is that her regions of declining manufacturing industry are given similar support for new development. If only Mrs. Thatcher had used her forensic skills and feminine wiles to win that support as part of the bargain, instead of defending a mythical sovereignty and opposing any increase in the Community's budget, much advantage could have been won for the British people. But then she did not believe in any subsidies, support systems or interventions in the "free" working of the market. Mr. Kinnock need respect no such dogmatic theology, but despite the Labour Party policies for social advancement and regional development in Europe, Mr. Kinnock's stance in relation to 1992 and to EMU has been to appear unconditionally enthusiastic, as a simple-minded political riposte to Mrs. Thatcher's reluctance. What is needed is not only proposals for the support of regions and groups which are harmed by the opening of the market, but a new look at sources of taxation for an expanded budget for development. Current reliance on VAT and food import levies is not enough if expenditure is to grow. Discussion of taxation policy is essential in all socialist parties where basic assumptions about progressive tax systems have been undermined by a decade of monetarist appeals to selfishness and private provision.

There is another reason for seeing an increasingly important role for the trade unions in Europe, which is perfectly well understood by more enlightened employers, especially in West Germany and Italy. This is that the competitive success of Japanese industrial organisation, using the new technology of electronic information systems and flexible automation, depends very much on establishing a co-operative partnership of management and workers, as well as a measure of co-operation to complement the competition between firms. I have already made the point that the strength of German trade unions has lain in their capacity to win higher wages through higher productivity, gained by positive participation in management planning. The new technology makes possible not only higher output per person in the productive process, but even greater savings in sourcing, distribution and marketing. All this, however, depends on team work, not only in management between design, production and marketing departments, but between management and workers. And, given the long tradition of trade unions in organising European workers, such co-operative working in Europe will have to be negotiated with the unions if it is to be effective. It is a striking fact that in the region of Europe which has most successfully adopted the new technology in design, production and marketing — Emilio Romagna in Italy — even mainly among small and medium-sized enterprises, the unions (and indeed communist-led local authorities) have been at the centre of this development. On a purely negative calculation, if working people are to strengthen their position in relation to the giant European companies after 1992, they will have to look to their unions. If they hope, further, to keep their jobs in face of Japanese competition, they will have to get their unions to work together on a European scale to take advantage of the opportunities presented by the technology of the new knowledge-based industries.

Trade unions, "greens" and communities: the need for education

Since the days of Marx's International, there has been no tradition of European trade union co-operation. The world-wide trade union movement was split by the Cold War. The international trade groups which continued to bring together national unions representing particular trades stood firmly on one side or the other of the Iron Curtain. When the European Trade Union Confederation was formed, it attracted the membership of most of the European trade union centres, although the French CGT held aloof and the Spanish CCOO was held at bay. As important as the meetings of these formal organisations have been, the informal meetings, mainly of shop stewards from plants in Britain and the continent of giant companies like Unilever, Kodak and Ford have been crucial. But political and national divisions remain deep-seated, and it has been only too easy for giant transnational companies to divide and conquer, in winning concessions from unions and their local communities when choosing the location of their plants. How well prepared, then, are the European unions for 1992?

To say that the unions are wholly unprepared for what will happen after 1992 would not be true; but compared with the preparations which industry has been making, their own efforts must appear to be quite inadequate. In Britain a number of individual unions like MSF and USDAW have drawn up awareness programmes, which fall well short of strategies for action. The TGWU has co-ordinated its Euro-MEP's into a European Parliamentary group, and has created a European Department with a senior official committed full-time. The TUC has proposed a strategy, but without timetables, specific responsibilities or resources assigned for its implementation. At the European level, the ETUC has issued a list of priorities for Community-wide action by unions. Union representatives have been sitting on joint committees for each of several industrial sectors together with the employers to discuss sectoral strategies. Joint committees for coal and steel, agriculture, sea fishing, road transport, air transport and maritime transport already exist. The Commission has facilitated joint meetings for metal working, textiles, sugar and brewing, construction, banking, and the retail trade. And the ETUC has been pressing for comprehensive coverage of all industrial sectors by such joint committees. But these meetings are moving exceedingly slowly, with strong resistance from British empoloyers backed by the British government, so that the adoption of common industrial policies, let alone a Social Charter, must seem a long way off. Meanwhile, mergers and take-overs among European companies proceed at a great pace, even among the giants themselves, in preparation for the day of the single market. While meetings between small groups of employers are easy to arrange, meetings between a wide range of national and industrial unions are only arranged with great difficulty. Such meetings cost a lot of money in airfares, accommodation and translation facilities; there is a lack among the unions of specialist officers with language skills, and a complete absence of education on the central issues involved, or of training in negotiation at the European level.

Besides the organised workers there are other groups which will be pressing for positive social policies to complement the opening of the single market and the establishment of monetary union. These are the "greens" and the minority national communities: the "greens" because they will want to see social provision and social regulation to control and reduce the waste and pollution which follow from atomised decisions in the market; the minorities because they can see in a federal structure some protection for their identity against the centralising tendencies of a unitary state. Pensioners and parents may also be regarded as groups with considerable mobilising potential in Europe. Co-operatives have already formed European linkages, which will be looked at in later chapters. Town twinning has become something more than an occasion for ceremonial wining and dining and some twinnings have resulted in economic collaboration. Women's organisations have been spreading across Europe. In the last resort, however, it will have to be the organised workers using their power as joint creators of wealth with technical management who can counter the tendency to uneven and unequal development. This tendency has always typified the working of the market, but today more than ever it reflects the domination of the market by a few giant companies. For, these are the market makers, while the rest find their position steadily weakening.

Trade unions are only strong if they can unite together, and if they truly represent the needs and aspirations of their members and their communities, and the wider society of which they are a part. Yet, sectional, regional and national differences will have to be subjected to the common interest if they are to be effective. Why should this happen? In a period of economic recession, nationalist and beggar-my-neighbour policies are much more likely to establish themselves. To understand that these are short-sighted and mistaken responses to a crisis implies a learning process which relates the facts of experience to general ideas. It is the strength of organised workers that they are capable of generalising their experience and taking action as a group to correct injustice and uneven development. But they need a forum, or many fora, in which to exchange experiences beyond their own work place and community, and thus to broaden their generalisation. There is here a key place for adult education.

What may be called the "movement" of adult education has followed the tide of demands made upon workers' organisations — swinging back and forth between self-improvement and social advance — the anti-fascist struggle before and during the Second World War, industrial recovery after the war, productivity bargaining and industrial democracy in the late 1960s and early 70s, defence of jobs in the community in the 1980s. The demand today is for a new internationalism. The powerful Workingmen's International, based in Britain in the 1860s, which Marx and Engels espoused, grew out of the attempt by European employers to exploit national differences and introduce cheap labour into manufacturing from reserves of displaced workers in the countryside. Differences in pay were not so great that unity could not be achieved. The same is true today, and a new international could be founded in Europe, but more than half the manufacturing workers in the world would be excluded. The transnational companies operate world-wide, and nothing less than a world-wide response to them will be required.

What could be begun in Europe is the habit of thinking internationally among organised workers. Trade unions were a British invention, the first International had its base in Britain. Is it beyond the capacity of British unions today to exorcise their insularity and begin to build bridges across the channel to their counterparts in Europe? Such a process of mutual engagement would take time, but it has to be begun now or British trade unionism will fade into a mere memory of past glories, of marches and banners and united actions in a dim period long ago. It will need new resources and new ways of thinking. It cannot just be a question of occasional top level meetings and solidarity action during disputes.

Traditional autonomous trade union bargaining will no doubt continue state by state, especially with local and regional government and smaller employers. But some common trade union structures will have to be developed to face up to the power of the giant European companies. This means that either the German metal workers union or the British engineering unions could come to organise both British and German workers in any particular company. There will still be major differences between national unions which employers can exploit. It may well be in the minds of German unions, in collusion with their employers and politicians, to be quite happy to export the higher social costs involved in the Social Charter, while withholding assistance to their British competitors in joint bargaining strategies. The story of the German unions holding back from the British campaign for a 35 hour week in the early 1980s, only to push it forward when it was convenient for their own economy , does not bode well for the future. But, the increasing commonality of membership of a single market and a single federation can only result in more understanding and will to co-operate — and that must be one of the main reasons for unions to support federation. At present, linkages tend to follow ideological rather than industrial or company lines. The AEU has made contact with IG Metall and MSF with the CGT. The TGWU says it feels more at ease culturally and ideologically with Italian unions than with those in Northern Europe. There is nothing wrong with this, but it may prove to be limiting for wider associations. Perhaps the catalyst of mass redundancies from arms conversion, or the next stage of manufacturing company mergers after 1992, will bring others together.

When the management of giant companies knows no national boundaries and state governments collude, workers' organisations cannot afford to remain in separate national groupings. The technical problems of travel and translation are not the real obstacle. What has to be overcome is a long tradition of narrow nationalism. But within the framework of existing adult and trade union education, it would be wise for those most concerned to communicate across national boundaries for advancing their several causes to begin a European network of adult education. This would link centres of study not only for developing languages skills but also for understanding different national approaches to social action and welfare provisions and their contribution to a European consensus. Without such preparation there can be no "social dialogue". It should be possible to draw upon the FORCE programme for financial resources, as well as for trade unions to begin to demand serious attention from the European Commission to their needs for finance to cover conference travel costs and translation facilities.

The links between organisations of labour in trade unions or small producers' associations and other popular organisations in local communities, among women, "greens" or ethnic minority groups, are of crucial importance in the internationalisation of democratic forces. The ethos of the market plus the salesmanship of giant companies divides us all up into anonymous producers and individualised consumers. Even organised producers and organised consumers in any region or locality can easily be divided and conquered by those who control the markets. What is needed is to find ways of bringing producers and consumers directly together again, as the market once did before the advent of large-scale production and mass consumption. Some possible ways of doing this through networking are explored in this book, so that as both producers and consumers we can exercise some real control over what is produced, what the conditions of production are, and what resources are used and their effect on the environment. Without such countervailing forces, the dynamic of capital accumulation will continue to encourage savings in direct costs to owners of capital in all their operations at whatever cost to human beings and to the environment. To discover such a critical mass of human energy to oppose that dynamic, we need to explore new ideas and experiment with new structures. So long as we do not forget our ties and obligations to the Third World, the new-found unity in

Europe offers a rare opportunity for innovation and exploration in political ideas and economic organisation.

References
Frank Blackaby, "A New Security for Europe", *European Labour Forum*, No.2, Autumn 1990.
M. Barratt Brown, *Economics of Imperialism*, Penguin, 1974; *From Labourism to Socialism* , Spokesman, 1972; *Europe 1992*, European Labour Forum, 1989.
Michael Best, *The New Competition*, Polity Press, 1990.
Ken Coates & Tony Topham, *Trade Unions in Britain*, Fontana, 1988.
P. Fairbrother & J. Waddington, "The Politics of Trade Unionism: Evidence and Theory" in *Capital & Class* No.4, Summer 1990.
Mike Press & Don Thòmson, *Solidarity for Survival: Trade Union Internationalism*, Spokesman, 1989.

CHAPTER 2

Only One World

It has for long been the received taxonomy to divide the world into three parts: the First, Second and Third Worlds. The political and economic collapse of Eastern Europe and the Soviet Union, which were in this rubric termed the Second World, has led to much self-congratulation in the First World of the developed industrial capitalist states. To sustain the self-satisfaction requires that the peoples of the First World should turn their eyes away and disown all responsibility for the steadily worsening economic conditions throughout most of the Third World. Apart from China, and perhaps Cuba and Libya, the Third World consists of political economies that are wholly integrated into the capitalist world market. China was generally seen in the West as being part of the Second World, but saw herself as the champion of the Third World. With this one exception, then, those who proclaim the successes of capitalism in the North must answer for its failures in the South. However good the claims that may be made for the economic growth of the four "Little Dragons" — South Korea, Taiwan, Hong Kong and Singapore — these four territories contain only sixty million of the 2,500 million people in the Third World (excluding China). The developed First World (including Japan) accounts for no more than one sixth of the world's population and less than a quarter of the capitalist total.

The causes of collapse in Eastern Europe

The most important fact to be recognised in the present world scene is that the collapse of Eastern Europe and the USSR is part of the same phenomenon as the collapse of the Third World. It has nothing to do with socialism in either the Second or Third World, whatever the claims that were once made for the Soviet Union and its border states. Socialism was a project about establishing democracy. Before this word was hi-jacked for a particular form of parliamentary government, it meant power for the people in place of the power of capital or land ownership or of a military caste. When the Party became the surrogate for the people, socialism was in effect abandoned, but an authoritarian bureaucracy planning from above did successfully carry through the first stages of industrialisation in the Soviet Union, just as it had done earlier in Germany and Japan and more recently in South Korea, the other "Little Dragons" and a few enclaves in other Third World countries. The problem of maintaining development has arisen in the later stages of industrialisation, where it appears that transferring capital from public to private ownership has been more successful than continuing public ownership. There is no doubt that in all cases it was bureaucratic control of state enterprises that proved most effective in the first stages. This is often clearly recognised in World Bank reports, although not in the Bank's prescriptions or those of the IMF for the practice of its debtors.

It is only right to make clear that the economic development of the Soviet Union after 1917, and of several of the other East European states after 1945, started from virtually Third World levels and reached almost the level of development of the industrialised First World by the late 1960s. The Soviet Union was after all the first country to launch a man into space. These were achievements which can only be paralleled by Japan and the four "Little Dragons". It could probably also be claimed that China had done better than either India or Pakistan in achieving the first stage of industrialisation and in ensuring a radical improvement in health and education. Authoritarian command economies have a proven track record in prosecuting a war and in the first stage of industrialisation. Why, then, did Eastern Europe, the Soviet Union and China falter thereafter? What was needed was to switch from extensive development — extra mines and factories — to intensive development — increased output per worker. One answer why this happened in Japan and South Korea and not in the Soviet Union is that the transfer of capital equipment from public to private ownership resulted in the private capitalists pursuing their natural aim of cutting labour costs in order to increase profits. Managers of public capital had no such incentive. They could do better for themselves by maximising the resources used up in production and there was no advantage to workers in increasing productivity when all were guaranteed employment.

This is the standard capitalist argument; and it has a strong element of truth in it, where no other motivation exists among workers or managers to reduce costs while retaining quality. Other motivations would have to comprise forms of self-management of enterprises and accountability to consumer requirements through market competition or consumer-producer networks. But these would challenge the power of the bureaucracy and the leading role of the Party. Japan and South Korea were for a long time single party states, but their governments encouraged competing private capitalists when state enterprises were privatised. Capitalist competition is of course no less wasteful both in the high levels of unemployment which the system tolerates and in the inequalities of income which the system generates, and which lead to periodic crisis and slump.

The nature of capitalist growth

How is it, then, that despite periodic crises and uneven development, capitalist growth has continued in the countries which were the first to industrialise and in those like Japan and the four "Little Dragons" which have followed after them? One answer which is often offered by critics of capitalist development is that the growth in a few countries has always been at the expense of the underdevelopment of the majority. Capitalist accumulation under British, and later, United States imperialism is said to have acted like a giant suction pump ever drawing profit from the periphery into the centre. If this were true, the pool would soon have run dry. In fact, new centres of capital accumulation — in the United States and Germany, and then in Japan and South Korea — have emerged, and others are emerging elsewhere. A second answer could be that countries like Japan and South Korea succeeded because, in effect, they cut themselves off for a time from the capitalist system of accumulation and only re-entered it when they were strong enough to compete. The Soviet Union also cut herself off from the capitalist world to develop her infant industries and so for a time did China. There is certainly much truth in this argument, but only countries which had huge natural resources like the Soviet Union, or seized the natural resources of their neighbours, as Japan did in China, could succeed in this way.

A third answer to the question of continuing capitalist growth is, quite simply, that the first comers had a great advantage in competitive strength which enabled them to keep ahead, and their leaders understood enough of the dangers of excessive concentration of wealth at the centre to take steps to redistribute this, albeit on their own terms. Thus, it could be argued that Britain in the hey-day of its power invested in the British dominions and that their growth made possible Britain's continued advance. Later, the United States not only invested in the territories where its sphere of influence ran, but gave aid to its friends, including even its competitors. Today, Japan and West Germany lend funds from their surpluses to the United States itself and to others who are in deficit. The result is uneven development — development of a few countries only, while many are left by the wayside — but it is a kind of development. The capitalist world economy and the trade between the several parts of it does continue to grow, sometimes faster, sometimes slower. What effect all this growth has on the environment and in using up non-renewable resources is something we shall have to look at later.

If this analysis of uneven development is correct, we should expect to find that countries which have not benefited from the investment, the loans and the aid of the first comers, have been falling steadily behind. These laggards would include all of the Second World and most of the Third World. Investment of capital from the advanced centres has been concentrated in cross-investment between the already developed countries. World Bank and IMF loans, and United States aid as well as investment, have been easily available to the already developed, much less easily and on much stricter terms to the developing. And, all too often, the aid for the developing was given on political terms, and was sometimes diverted into the private hands of those through whom the aid was channeled, the giant companies' order books, and even the private pockets of rulers like the Shah of Iran or the Marcoses of the Philippines; and so flowed back again into real estate in Florida or Hawaii or bank accounts in Switzerland, in ways that make the peculations of Honecker and even Ceaucescu seem like the merest peccadilloes.

The largest historic transfer of funds from any one country to the aid of others was the United States aid under the Marshall Plan provided to Western Europe and Japan at the end of the Second World War. The USSR, Eastern Europe and China were excluded from this transfer, although the war damage on their territories was far worse than elsewhere. That all these peoples who were excluded recovered from the war as well as they did, without outside aid, is a tribute to the efforts that their regimes inspired and the planning system that they adopted, although this became a brake on their development at a later stage.

Uneven development in one world

Starting their industrialisation later, with greater war-time destruction in two world wars and without access to United States aid or international funding, it was not surprising that the Second World and most of the Third World should have fallen behind the technological advances of the First World, although for a time they kept up with, and even exceeded, their growth in output. The crunch came in the 1970s when those countries without oil reserves had to borrow against their reserves of other primary products to go on paying for imported oil at hiked up prices, and those which had oil reserves borrowed against their oil to buy new plant and equipment from the First World, so as to accelerate their industrial development. When the price of oil and of other primary products collapsed in the early 1980s, the countries of both the Second and the Third World found themselves loaded with a great incubus of debt owed to the First World; and, while prices of their exports were falling, the prices in the First World both of their manufactured goods and of money itself were rising.

As debts could not be repaid and were rescheduled, equally by Third World and by Second World countries, the size of the debt grew to reach a figure three times the original sums that had been borrowed. The First World has for the time being greatly benefited from obtaining its oil and primary products from the Third World at lower prices and receiving vastly increased remittances of funds. For, the fact is that since 1983, despite rescheduling, far from aid and loans flowing out from the First World to the Second and Third as before, the flow has been reversed. A net outward flow of $40 billions a year at the end of the 1970s has been replaced by a far greater net inward flow at the end of the 1980s: the equivalent of several Marshall plans in reverse. This is typical of the way capitalism generated inequality. "To whom that hath shall be given, and from whom that hath not shall be taken away even that which they have"; and the inequalities have grown equally inside both the First and Third Worlds. Only an elite, large in the First World and small in the Third, can afford the whole range of consumer goods that modern technology can provide. But such accumulation of wealth at one pole and poverty at the other is in the long run self-defeating. The impoverished people of the Third World can no longer buy the products of the First World. Like Midas, the rich cannot eat the gold with which they have surrounded themselves and must die if they do not redistribute it. One of the great attractions for First World capitalists of the opening up of the Eastern European and Soviet Second World market is that there the inequalities of income are not so great as in the Third World. The market will be that much wider. Average purchasing power, while below that in the First World, is well above that in the Third.

This picture of inequalities generated worldwide by the accumulation of capital drawing in wealth far beyond the First World from the Third World and Second World too, is hardly the picture of two competing blocs fighting for supremacy, which we are usually presented in the propaganda of capitalists and their opponents alike. It is much more a picture of one world system of accumulation built up over the centuries, from which it is possible but exceedingly difficult to escape. The Soviets, the Chinese, the East Europeans, the Cubans and Sandinistas and many others have all tried and failed. The Japanese and the four "Little Dragons" succeeded but with massive support from Marshall Aid and United States investment, and from United States military expenditure in the Korean and Vietnam wars. By contrast, the Vietnamese were left with a totally devastated country and a trade blockade to overcome.

Could not Eastern Europe and the Soviet Union now recover with financial support from the First World and so ensure the recovery at the same time of an ailing First World? There is no doubt, judging from the earlier experience of Marshall Aid that this could be done, but it would require a quite massive increase in the funds that are now on offer, something up to the level of Marshall Aid, and with the Soviet Union included. On present levels of promised aid it is only Eastern Germany that will be incorporated into the capitalist system as an equal partner. Elsewhere, in Eastern Europe and the Soviet Union the most likely future scenario will be similar to that in Brazil or Mexico — an end to egalitarianism and the development of a deep division between a minority on high levels of income able to buy all the products of Western technology, and a majority providing a new reserve of cheap and skilled labour for the factories of giant companies translated from Japan, the United States and Western Germany and from other advanced industrial centres.

In such a scenario the redistribution of income would not be enough to hold off the gathering crisis of the global system of capital accumulation. For, what we are witnessing today, on a scale never seen before, is an accumulation of capital by a small number of giant companies and of national balances in a still smaller number of nation states, while the overwhelming number of companies and governments and households are in deficit. With such inequalities there are no openings for investment in new productive capacity. The accumulated wealth goes into mergers and take-overs and unproductive speculation. At some stage the bubble must burst. When something like this happened before, in the 1870s and in the first and third decades of this century, international war served to wipe out the surpluses as well as much existing plant, and thus the cumulative process could start up again. Today the option of world war is ruled out by the finally destructive nature of modern weapons. Those who believe that in the chaos of an economic crisis a new socialist order can be born should recall that it was fascism which emerged from the crisis last time. In the interest of all, something needs positively to be done to avert a crisis of quite overwhelming proportions. To find solutions we have to look in detail at the problem, first of all of the debt crisis.

The East European debt
The total foreign debt of the USSR and East Europe is around $180 billions. That is what they owe to Western governments and banks; it is almost double what it was in 1980, since which time interest charges have trebled. The debt amounts to almost 70 per cent of these countries' annual exports. Since about a half of their exports go to each other, it is more meaningful to say that servicing the debt takes over a third of their hard currency export earnings every year. In the case of Poland the proportion is over 100 per cent; in the case of the USSR about 20 per cent. The figure for the GDR lay at the upper end of the range, but it was offset by aid from West Germany and special trade with West Germany equivalent to some $3 to $4 billions, about a fifth of the East German debt. For Czechoslovakia the figure is at the lower end of the range; for the others about 40 per cent is the average.

The USSR and the East European countries increased their exports from 7.7 per cent of the world total in 1980 to 9.0 per cent in 1987, but in 1988 this figure fell back to 8.1 per cent. They increased their balance of payments surplus with the outside world from 1980 to 1987, but this was partly the result of reducing their imports. Since 1985 exports in total have been raised by a third, but only by 20 per cent to outside countries. They have not been able to raise the prices of their exports during this period, while the prices of manufactured imports from the West have risen very sharply, by over 40 per cent. Soviet exports were badly hit by the fall in oil and gas and mineral prices in 1984. Other commodity prices and particularly food prices affecting East European exports have also been falling, while East European manufactured exports have had to be subsidised to hold their place in highly competitive markets.

The most serious part of the debt problem facing the USSR and Eastern Europe is the same as that facing Third World countries which have large debts and have suffered rising interest rates and declining commodity prices. This is that, with no new lending taking place, a reverse transfer of funds occurs — from the poorer to the richer — i.e. in this case from East Europe to the West. This is most obvious in the case of Poland which has annual debt service obligations greater than all its foreign exchange earnings. So long as this is occurring, and it has been occurring for nearly a decade, it is impossible for the poorer countries to find the resources to invest in the new plant and equipment that they must have from the richer countries to develop their economies and to produce goods of a quality that the West will accept as imports. The subsidising of labour-intensive exports — of clothing, shoes, furniture and the like — so as to sell them in Western markets simply adds another burden onto the Eastern economies and results in shortages in the shops and rising rates of inflation.

False solutions

It is this reverse flow of funds which renders useless all proposals for tackling the debt problem by rescheduling only. The problem is simply postponed and aggravated as interest charges accumulate. This again would not be so serious if there were any chance of the debtor countries developing their productive capacity to compete in Western markets. East Germany alone of the East European countries had, through its trading links with West Germany, been able to maintain a capital investment programme that was anywhere near to that in the countries of Western Europe. Rescheduling debt without new lending also renders useless the forms of economic conditionality which the IMF imposes on borrowers. The usual conditions required are that the government of the indebted country should cut back public spending and cease subsidising inefficient industries. Unless the net flow of funds is once again reversed, so that the poor countries have resources for new capital investment, which means capital goods imports, there will only be a massive rise in unemployment and inevitable economic and social disorder as the result. One solution proposed for Third World countries is that debt should be converted into equity holdings in local industry. Quite apart from the political issues involved in the case of state owned enterprises in the USSR and East Europe, there must be some doubt whether there are industries there which Western capital would be interested in owning. The possibility of a conversion of debt into ownership rights in the new enterprise zones in the USSR opens up an unanswered question about the capacity or desire of the Soviet government to absorb a major element of the Western capitalist system into its own economic structures.

One obvious solution to the debt problem might seem to be that debts should simply be written off by the lender or reneged on by the borrower. Most Western banks have been engaged in the last few years, with some governmental support, in building up reserves against such eventualities. This means, of course, that the funds going into such reserves are not available for new lending, so that once again there is no solution to the basic problem of uneven development. Milton Friedman has proposed that banks should price the worth of their debts in the market to determine their value and then write them down to that value. The lower the value the higher would be the rate of interest for new lending. IMF conditions would not then be required as the market would settle the matter. It probably would: countries in debt would stop borrowing as well as default on past debts, because the rates of interest would be punitive.

A true solution

These so-called solutions address only one half of the debt problem — the Western banks' holdings of vast unserviceable debt in their balance sheets. Unless the other half of the problem — the need for new funds for investment, to produce the goods to pay back the debts — is also addressed, the problem is insoluble. Without new flows of funds the existing debts must become worthless. How then is the existing debt on the books of the banks to be dealt with and new lending made available? Only government action can assure this. Certainly, no individual Western bank can on its own. Nor, in effect, can any individual Western government, unless it takes on only the debt of one country, as Western Germany is taking on Eastern Germany's financing. For anything more, a group of Western governments will be required to supply some form of guarantee — somewhat like export credit guarantees — of the interest payments on new lending. This would be in place of the present government support given to banks by way of tax concessions for writing off old debts. A condition of the guarantee would be the writing down of doubtful debts, but the objective would be to restart the flow of funds from the richer to the poorer countries. Guarantees would have to avoid specific time limits so as to allow for debtors to improve their payments balances. The amounts guaranteed would have to be at least equal to the present level of reverse transfers. Even if the same guarantees were applied to all debts — Third World and Second World — the sum of about $50 billions which would be needed is only about one-tenth of the normal annual growth of the incomes of the rich countries and much less than the annual expansion of credit made available inside their own economies.

It has been suggested in the financial press that there is some current difference of view over the East European debt problem between the IMF and the World Bank. How far the World Bank is moving towards a solution of the debt problem along the lines suggested here is not clear, but the difference from the IMF "solution" can be simply summarised. IMF conditionality is designed to extract transfers in the short term from the (poor) debtors to the (rich) creditors. These proposals are by contrast designed to ensure transfers from the rich countries to the poor debtors, so that they can cover their debt interest in the short term and achieve the long term viability of their economies. If the current economic crisis in the USSR and Eastern Europe does not have its origins in the growth of debt to the West, it has certainly been seriously aggravated by it. No solutions to this crisis are possible without a solution to the debt problem. And it is very evident that the political crisis in the East cannot be solved without solving the economic crisis.

What the European Community should do now

At a time when the Soviet and East European peoples are looking more openly than for many years for support and co-operation from Western Europe, a response to the debt problem must come very high on the agenda of Western statesmen. For democratic socialists such support and co-operation are absolutely crucial. It would be only too easy in seeking short-term political gain to allow advantage to be taken of the economic weakness in the East. Just to rescue Eastern Germany in a reunified Greater Germany is not enough. In the long run, the West must be the loser too, if economic recovery is not assured throughout the East. Social disorder and economic breakdown are no recipe for peaceful or democratic development. It is not possible to exaggerate the extent of such disorder if there is no sign of a way out of the impasse, and instead of economic reconstruction only economic destruction follows at the behest of the IMF.

While President Gorbachev is speaking of one single European home, the time is evidently ripe for genuine measures of East-West co-operation. A solution to the debt problem has to be the first step towards building that common home. Socialists in the East and West of Europe will find no solace in the continuing uneven development that results from unregulated market forces. Inequalities are bound to worsen inside the Western countries themselves as well as between them and the East, unless measures are taken to check the polarisation of wealth and poverty. Expanding, instead of contracting, purchasing power in the East (and in the South) means expanding employment in the West. UNCTAD officials have calculated that a 25 per cent reduction in interest payments on the outstanding debt of highly indebted countries would, with associated measures, raise these countries' net imports by some \$18 billions. About two-thirds of these imports would be of investment goods and that would restore 70 per cent of the cuts in capital goods imports from the developed market economies effected since the early 1980s. Similar proportions would be involved in a reduction of the debt liability of Eastern Europe and the restoration of net lending. The world economy, like peace, is indivisible.

A new Marshall Plan for Eastern Europe

In current discussion of something like a new Marshall Plan, this time for Eastern and not Western Europe, there appears to be an assumption that this would appropriately be administered by the IMF and under IMF rules. No such requirement was made of the Western European governments in 1948-50, and it is unlikely that US aid then would have been anywhere near so effective if it had been. The East European countries' current burden of debt and of payments deficits are similar to the dollar deficits of Western Europe after the Second World War. The IMF rules require cuts in public and personal spending by recipients of aid so that import demand falls and exports are encouraged. At the same time, currencies are to be devalued to make imports more expensive for the debtor countries and their exports cheaper. IMF regimes of this sort have been wholly unsuccessful among Third World debtor countries, whose outstanding debt has continued to grow as increased exports, even including their inheritance of tropical forest, have failed to keep up with interest payments. Indeed, it is not too much to say that IMF policies have been an unmitigated disaster for the whole world, and not just for the debtor countries.

It can hardly be supposed that the same policies will fare better in Eastern Europe. It is often claimed by the monetarists that there is no alternative, and that financial discipline — removing all subsidies and opening the economy to the world market — will alone create the conditions for efficient enterprise. The results may not be absolutely disastrous for a developed economy with a strong safety net of social security provisions. Such measures, however, cannot be applied to most of Eastern Europe, where there is no such safety net. It should be recalled that for seven years after Mrs Thatcher introduced financial discipline in Britain, state expenditure as a proportion of the National Product continued to rise — to meet the payments to the unemployed. And, as we are learning to our cost, the cuts in public spending on goods and services have left the UK with a greatly impaired infrastructure of roads, railways, water supplies, sewerage, education and hospital services. It will be far worse in Eastern Europe if aid is only made available, that is for writing off debt and for foreign currency purchases, on condition that public and personal consumption are sharply cut back.

This is where the lessons learnt from the Marshall Plan can usefully be recalled. First of all, the sums involved were massive by any count. Over $17 billions of aid (some $200 billions at present values) were provided over the three years 1948-50. Nearly as much again had been supplied in the previous two years in non-military grants and loans. It was a massive transfer of wealth. The recipients were the Western European nations and Japan. It is a primary point of importance for Eastern Europe's condition today that the USSR and the countries under Soviet tutelage were excluded from Marshall Aid. Molotov had come with a team of sixty experts to the Paris conference in 1947 to discuss the continuation of United Nations aid after the UN Relief and Rehabilitation programme ended, and had been met by Bevin's proposal to bring the Marshall offer under an Organisation for European Economic Co-operation, which would co-ordinate national recovery plans with officials of the US Economic Co-operation Agency (ECA) to advise. Molotov withdrew, protesting at what he saw as a blatant attempt to impose United States hegemony. Left-wing members of the Labour Party like Zilliacus bitterly attacked Bevin's exclusive tactics, but Stalin was suspicious also of the United Nations, which was the only alternative to an OEEC. The Cold War had begun, and those of us who were in the UNRRA, and had hoped to find further employment with the UN Economic Commission for Europe, returned home from Geneva disappointed. It is an ironic tragedy that Poland was at that time the most insistent on a UN solution.

Public expenditure — the key to recovery
The second lesson to be learned from the Marshall Plan is that, while the officials of the US ECA undoubtedly represented the policies of the US government and the interests of US industry, the several European governments did prepare their own plans. With ECA advice on placing orders for US equipment, they used the aid and counterpart funds in their own different ways. How the aid was used is not widely recognised. The British government's response was to apply the funds to eliminating its dollar debts and to strengthening the position of the Sterling Area, which was all that was left of Britain's colonial empire. This was not enough to prevent a second devaluation of sterling, but some funds were used for investment in industry, especially by United States' firms. Since, at the war's end, British manufacturers were the only source of supply for machinery and transport equipment outside of the USA, they had no difficulty, especially with the pound devalued, in selling anything they could produce. Exports soon exceeded imports and the need for aid diminished. The aid had not, however, been applied to the total overhaul and restructuring of British industry which was required after a decade of slump and another decade of war. British government links with the City, even the Labour

governments' worship of the pound sterling, are generally blamed; but management cannot be exonerated nor the trade unions. Once again, as in the 1900s, it was not the strength of the unions that was the problem, but the weakness of union leaders in restraining wage demands which would have forced employers to step up their capital investment. The continuing uncompetitive condition of British industry to this day goes back to these earlier failures.

It was quite otherwise on the continent of Europe. Large left-wing parties, some sharing power and others in Opposition, were ensuring that Marshall Aid funds were devoted to industrial reconstruction and regional development. In France, the availability of counterpart funds from Marshall Aid made possible the indicative planning framework which carried the French economy forward from the total stagnation of the 1930s and 1940s to its dynamic growth in the 1950s and 1960s. In Italy, two successive long-term economic plans — from 1948 to 1953 and from 1955 to 1964 — were based on the use of Marshall Aid funds for public expenditure in the poorer regions, and for modernisation through public enterprise groups. In West Germany, Marshall Aid was channeled through a Public Reconstruction Loans Corporation and, far from the German "miracle" owing its origin to the freedom given for spontaneous private enterprise, the crucial role was played by the public authorities in selecting and fostering industrial and regional projects. Most of this was clearly understood and thoroughly documented in Thomas Balogh's *Planning for Progress*, 1963, and Andrew Shonfield's *Modern Capitalism*, 1965; and fully reviewed in Jaques Delors' and Stuart Holland's *Beyond Central Planning*, 1978.

It all makes a nonsense of the monetarists' claims for the freeing of market forces in income distribution and for the reduction of public expenditure as the proper guidelines for recovery. Direct state intervention in social redistribution and industrial restructuring, combined with US public aid, followed by US private investment, sustained 30 years of expanding world trade and output up to 1973. Since then, 16 years of monetarism and blind faith in market forces have resulted in world-wide recession, mass unemployment and international debts amounting to over 3,000 billion dollars.

The *laissez-faire* alternative

What should the lesson be for the peoples of the Soviet Union and Eastern Europe emerging from single Party rule, enshrined in a corrupt Party leadership and sustained by a secret police and the suppression of all freedom of expression, association, travel or demonstration? It must not be assumed that they should abandon all planning and public provision and open every aspect of life to the free reign of market forces, let alone attempt to encourage private enterprise by allowing private ownership of capital and the exploitation of labour. This was not how Western Europe recovered after 1945. Eastern Europe and the Soviet Union start with two great advantages — a highly educated population and strong egalitarian traditions. Those who rightly recoil from stories of the wealth and corruption of the Communist Party elite, now revealed in the East, should be aware of the infinitely greater wealth of the industrial barons of the West (Lord Hanson with an annual income of over £2 million) and the veritable archipelago of capitalist corruption that links the production and final sale of the Third World's commodities, its minerals in particular.

The great weaknesses of the Soviet economy, and those of the other East European countries, lie not only in the out-of-date industrial plant but in the absence of an infrastructure of roads and railways and communications, and of repair shops, wholesale and retail networks. Above and beyond these weaknesses stands the grotesquely top-heavy government apparatus which attempts to decide and supervise everything and is, as a result, unable to exercise just those acts of intervention and support which the economic agents, both enterprises and individuals, need for effective performance. The end result of these advantages and disadvantages is that, if Eastern Europe's debt burden were to be eased and its economies exposed to Western capitalism, then the large transnational companies would undoubtedly find a skilled labour force that could be trained and a new market for the consumer goods produced by modern technology, of which the people complain that they have been starved. But to what end?

To avoid the development in the East of a model of dependent capitalism, like Brazil, will require not only firm resistance from the Soviet and East European governments to western capital's blandishments, but effective control over the aid and other funds made available, so that these are actually spent on regional development, improving the infrastructure, and modernising manufacturing industry. Brazil should indeed provide the warning. In ten years time the Soviet Union could be ruled by a military dictatorship, its forests and rich raw materials laid waste to pay its debts and those of its East European allies, cheap labour in its factories producing consumer goods for Western transnational companies; while a small elite in the big cities and the Baltic states, and in Hungary and Czechoslovakia, lives at Western standards, the vast mass of the people fall back into poverty and perennial hunger.

In the long run this is not a scenario for self-sustaining development of the world, even the First World. If the environment survives and frustrated expectations do not boil over into violent military exchanges involving nuclear weapons, the capacity to produce must more and more come into conflict with the failure of consumption to expand in a grossly unequal society. It cannot be too strongly emphasised that the success of Marshall Aid was that it was used for social redistribution as well as for industrial reconstruction. This implies a key role for public intervention in regulating the use of market mechanisms; and the scale of economic activity today requires that this shall be international. The hope must be that, together with the Soviet Union and Eastern Europe, the European Community could merge their traditions to build a true social market. The need for public intervention is all the greater because of the profligate waste of non-renewable resources and the assault on the environment which have marked economic development everywhere in the last fifty years.

European or world economic order?
The euphoria generated in the West by the collapse of the centrally planned economies in the East has led to certain assumptions being made which may well prove to be mistaken. The first is that with the strengthening of the European Community's Economic and Monetary Union, and the probable inclusion of Eastern Germany, the other Eastern European states can be associated in an expanded EFTA, possibly including also the Baltic nations, but with the USSR excluded. The second is that, while facing up to the USA and Japan, a much strengthened Europe, not to say a "Fortress Europe", can afford largely to neglect the needs and interests and contribution of the Third World including China.

In such a scenario, the obstinate fact will remain that the Third World, including China and with the Soviet Union, comprise together some 80 per cent of the world's population and 70 per cent of the cultivable land, even if only 30 per cent of industrial output and international trade. Moreover, these territories contain 60 per cent of the oil and gas reserves, and proportions ranging from 60 per cent to 80 per cent of the world's key minerals. In some of these the Soviet Union alone supplies more than half of the world's total. In the light of these facts, it is evidently impossible to exclude their representation, and particularly that of the Soviet Union, from the discussions leading to a new economic order, even for Europe.

It may be argued that the giant transnational companies from Europe, North America and Japan have nearly all the sources of oil and gas and minerals that exist outside of the Soviet Union and

China, already tied into their vertically integrated operations. But that assumes the continued acquiescence in these operations of the workers and peoples of those countries where these resources are found. Recent events in the Gulf and in southern Africa should not encourage a too-easy assumption of this continuation. Nor should the authoritarian rule so recently re-established in China be expected to imply a necessarily accommodating response to Western interest in markets and investment in that quarter, any more than should the democratic developments in the USSR imply an alternative market for the West to a stagnating Third World, but for how long?

A third assumption in the current euphoria is that the instability of the Western economic system will not worsen as the result of the enormous build-up of credit and debt, not only in the United States and UK trade deficits and the debts owed to Western banks by governments in the Third World and in Eastern Europe too, but the mass of debt accumulated inside the industrialised countries themselves. The ratio of debt-to-assets is like a pack of cards built up on a narrow base. It can collapse only too easily if just one card is pulled away. Perhaps one card can be replaced, one collapse made good, but the danger is that more than one should go, not one bank failure but several, not one giant company bankrupt but many. While the assets grow, all may be well, but what has been feeding the growth over the last decade has been the steadily falling prices of inputs — most of them fuel and raw materials from the Third World. In the short run, this improves the terms of trade of the industrialised countries and gives them strength, together with the flow of funds from the Third World debt repayments.

What will be the effect of the incorporation into the world system of Eastern Europe, with or without the Soviet Union? Eastern Europe offers some new markets and much skilled labour. The Soviet Union is an even larger market and has massive resources of fuels and minerals, from which it has been supplying Eastern Europe at well below world prices. What happens if Soviet prices are increased to world levels and Eastern Europe looks westward for more of its trade? It seems most probable that in the current recession of world demand the two events will cancel each other out: the higher Soviet prices and the wider availability of new sources of fuel and minerals in the world market. But if the USSR were to join OPEC and follow a restrictive policy, oil prices could harden at Gulf crisis levels. Even in the absence of restrictions, it would be wise for the West to ensure that Soviet actions should ease rather than further disturb the uncertainties of the current economic situation. This implies the creation of a framework which includes Soviet supplies and Soviet markets in the triangle of trade between East and West and South.

Soviet reliance in her trade exchanges on exports of primary products serves to emphasise her affinity to the Third World of the South. The more the Soviet Union is elbowed out of the "common European home", the more she will be driven to assume, as Lenin once predicted, the mantle of Third World leadership, possibly, and more threateningly for the West, in unison with China. Is this what European statesmen want? In spite of all the propaganda from certain quarters, Soviet arms have played a very minor role in Third World revolutions. Mr Gorbachev has sought to follow another route towards righting political injustice and economic inequality than the way of armed struggle. It would be an act of statesmanship to meet him half way. As every day passes, we are reminded by the running down of non-renewable natural resources and by the threat to the human environment that the world is one world. There is no future for mankind in rival groups trying to carve out separate corners of it as their special preserve.

Global collapse or recovery?

In all the excitement engendered in the West by the economic and political collapse of the East, there is some danger that inadequate attention is being paid to the possibility that economic collapse in the West is near at hand. Stock Exchange prices are drifting downwards with fears of higher interest rates, further falls in commodity prices and the unrest in the Soviet Union. The falls are world-wide, affecting even West Germany and Japan, as well as the USA and UK. The particular weakness of the British economy is being revealed in falling output, rising inflation and a massive balance of payments deficit. But the crisis is global, and in many ways similar to the 1930s slump.

The crisis takes the form of an unequal distribution of money — too much in the hands of the few, too little in the hands of the many. Money demand fails to correspond to expanding productive capacity. The dollar is no longer available as an ever-expanding world money. The United States' deficit indeed has grown so large that the US government has had to adopt policies to cut back on global spending. There is, however, no other world money. Japan and West Germany, which both have surpluses that they have been lending to the USA, do not either of them offer big enough markets to replace United States hegemony. The UK is now a very minor economic power with a very large deficit. The European Community's twelve states together have the economic power (40 per cent of world exports compared with the US and Japan's 10 per cent each), but they do not yet have a single money. It will not be enough, however, for the European Community to form an Economic and Monetary Union and make some links with EFTA and Eastern Europe and the Community's African, Caribbean and Pacific associated states. The crisis is a global challenge and only a global response will be adequate. It may have been *folie de grandeur* that motivated Mrs Thatcher's resistance to taking the UK into EMU, but there are real problems for any weak economy in such a union unless there is a wider element of expansion built in.

Without a world money and with no fixed exchange rates world-wide, we are back to the situation of the 1930s but with a difference. The pound sterling then lost its position as the basis of the world's money. After the crash of 1929, each nation state which had the power to do so, tried to protect its economy by beggar-my-neighbour policies of protection and currency devaluation, combined with cuts in public spending. World trade and world price levels fell steadily, so that the value of world trade exchanges in January 1933 was just one-third of what it had been in January 1929. Today, after the crash of 1987, each nation state which had the power to do so through deploying its reserves, has tried to protect its currency. Although unemployment is high and output is stagnant, and world trade growth slowed down, prices have been rising in all the major industrial nations. Each nation state seeks to administer its money supply, but all pretend that money prices are set in an uncontrolled market.

Why the difference from the 1930s?
In the First World of industrial nation states today the power of both labour and capital has been able to resist any attempt at a massive deflation by governments reducing the level of public spending. Such spending by nation states now accounts for around 50 per cent of national incomes, compared with only 30 per cent in the 1930s. Governments, instead of competitively devaluing their currencies, have competitively protected them by offering higher interest rates to attract and retain mobile capital. The weaker the economy the higher the interest rate has had to be. The stronger economies have survived, although output has been stagnant. Disaster has struck the poorer and most indebted countries — in Eastern Europe and the Third World. They have no resources and have been unable to protect their currencies or the prices of their pimary products, which are all they have to offer on the world market, but they have had to pay the high rates of interest of the rich countries they borrowed from. Every one per cent fall in the

index of commodity prices means a loss of $1 billion in Third World purchasing power, and that, of course, in the end works back into lost jobs in the First World. For the manufacturers in the rich First World rely on their exports to the Third World for 20 per cent of the market, plus another 10 per cent in the Second World (that is of the USSR, China and Eastern Europe).

Since all governments are now trying to protect their currencies, no one national currency, not even the currency of one of the strongest economies, can become a world money. This is because to keep a currency strong it has to be both sought after and kept relatively scarce. The Bretton Woods institutions — World Bank, IMF and GATT — were all founded on the basis of a gold-backed United States dollar, which was a recognition of US economic hegemony. Even when the gold link was cut, the dollar was still trusted until there were just too many dollars floating around, and the dominant position of the US economy was under challenge. To decide what should be done now, we need to go back to the original proposals which Keynes submitted to the Bretton Woods meetings. They were based on the assumption, not of United States hegemony as it emerged at the end of the war, but of a relatively equal partnership of the USA and the UK and equal places for other major powers in the future, especially the USSR and China, France and the defeated powers, Germany and Japan. Now that we are back again with no single dominant world power, Keynes's proposals become peculiarly relevant. Money could be administered to a common end, instead of the separate ends of many states.

A new Bretton Woods

In order to avoid the beggar-my-neighbour problems with national currencies, Keynes proposed a non-national currency, which he called "BANCOR" to serve as the world money. This would be backed by the gold and currency reserves of all the national governments and would be managed by international civil servants as bankers. The IMF, the World Bank and an International Trade Organisation were to operate also as genuinely international agencies with access to enough funds for them to be effective, and to act without political strings. The US Government would have none of this; and in the event, the world's trade expanded far ahead of the world's gold and dollar reserves and IMF quotas because the US continued to buy more than she sold and ran a deficit that steadily expanded. An attempt was made in the late 1970s to introduce Special Drawing Rights (SDRs) in order to increase an international source of liquidity, but these were limited to quite small sums. A proposal made in 1964 at the first UNCTAD meeting by Professors Hart, Kaldor and Tinbergen to add in the commodity reserves of the Third World countries was not accepted. As a result, by the mid-1980s the total of all gold and other reserves was only enough to finance about two months of the world's current imports. IMF quotas and SDRs contributed about three weeks to this. It had been Keynes's intention that IMF quotas should cover something approaching a quarter, i.e. about three months, of current trade. Only the US dollar kept trade moving until it too became suspect as the US lost its hegemony.

With no single hegemonic power in the capitalist world as we know it, the Group of Seven — the USA, Japan, West Germany, Canada, France, Italy and the UK — now hold regular summit meetings. Apart from resolving to reduce interest rates and inflation and maintain exchange rates, they do nothing to create a new framework of world finance, not even writing off the debts of the world's poorest countries. Who then can act? It is clear that the United States can do nothing on its own, given its deficit of $120 billions and its falling competitiveness. Japan, which has the competitive edge and a surplus of $80 billions, is quite prepared to lend to the US government and to invest in the USA and elsewhere, but it has only a relatively small market (six per cent of world imports) which it seems most unwilling to open further. Despite showing some interest in Eastern Europe, Japan's main preoccupation appears to be in the Pacific Basin. This leaves the European Community, which includes four of the leading industrial "Group of Seven".

A long-term initiative from the European Community
The European Community has the power to act in the long term interest of all. The European Economic and Monetary Union is a step forward towards united action. This implies not only accommodating the UK, but reaching new agreements with other European states, East and West, and coming to terms with Japan and the USA. All these steps could much more easily be taken, and a framework built for a wider relationship with the Third World, if the Community were to launch a major initiative to establish a new Bretton Woods agreement. The SDR already exists as the basis for a world money. The management structure will have to provide for the new economic powers of Japan, the European Community itself, and the USSR and China. The bargaining power of these Second World nations and of the Third World will need to be increased by including their contribution of a commodity currency reserve along with the gold and hard currency reserves of the First World. This will be needed both for resolving past debt claims and for

guaranteeing future claims on financial resources. An International Trade Organisation will be needed to complement a revised IMF and World Bank, to replace GATT and to strengthen UNCTAD and its Common Fund for encouraging world-wide measures of trade development under popular control.

It may seem quite bizarre to be suggesting that the European community should take the lead in world trade development, when it protects its farmers and labour intensive industries behind a great wall of levies and tariffs and subsidies. The collapse of the GATT discussions of agricultural protection at the end of 1990 appears to indicate a quite uncompromising resistance to opening the gates of the fortress. But this is because the GATT machinery is concerned only with removing negative restraints on trade expansion. As such it is, as an Indian delegate once described it, a "one way street" down which the most technically advanced producers can drive. These are the giant companies of the North and West, including the agro-industry producers of food. Others coming up from the South are pushed to the side and even forced to abandon their progress. The logic of the GATT method of freeing trade is ironically that it encourages the formation of blocs. If the round of GATT talks that began in Uruguay four years ago in the end breaks down, the result will be a movement towards three or four separate trading blocs built around the strongest producers — the American continent dominated by the USA, the European continent dominated by Germany, the Pacific ring dominated by Japan, and a marginalised Africa and Southern Asia. Since only one half of the world's trade consists in exchanges inside these blocs and the other half takes place between them, this must mean a disastrous decline in world trade. The European bloc would be by far the largest with half the total to start with, but only half of that consists of intra-trade exchanges. Thus, Europe has not only the greater possibility but the greatest interest in stimulating world-wide measures of trade development.

After the next major financial crisis in the Western world, measures of this kind will have, in the end, to be taken to construct a new world order out of the ruins, but there could be a long and most dangerous interim period of instability, disorder, violence and military "solutions", such as followed after the last great crash of the 1930s. It would greatly increase the chances of survival of the human race if these measures of reconstruction could be begun now, so as to ward off the next collapse and launch a programme of recovery. The alternative of challenging the role of money, ending the rule of capital, wiping out all credit and debt must be regarded as a somewhat distant prospect for which nothing less than a global revolution would be required. In the meantime, we can but seek to bring money and banking and trade as far as is possible under democratic systems of control. If the governments of states will not act then the people through their Parliaments and the United Nations will have to take the first steps and demand that action is taken now before it is too late.

References
Peter Berger, *The Capitalist Revolution*, Wildwood House, 1987.
Rhys Jenkins, *Transnational Corporations and Uneven Development*, Methuen, 1987.
H. Lever & C. Huhne, *Debt and Danger*, Penguin, 1987.
Peter Gowan, "Western Economic Diplomacy and the New Eastern Europe", *New Left Review*, No.182, July-Aug. 1990.
Konni Zilliacus, *I Choose Peace*, Penguin 1950.
T. Balogh, *Planning for Progress*, Weidenfeld, 1962.
A. Shonfield, *Modern Capitalism*, Macmillan, 1965.
Stuart Holland, *Beyond Central Planning*, Weidenfeld, 1978.
M. Gorbachev, *Perestroika*, Collins, 1987.
UNCTAD, *Trade and Development Report for 1989*, UNCTAD.
Clive Robinson, *Hungry Farmers*, Christian Aid, 1989.

CHAPTER 3

Should we all be paid in Ecus?

Correcting inequalities

How can European Union help to correct the growing inequalities of wealth and income? The report submitted to the Socialist Group of the European Parliament from the Association for Applied Research in the European Community (ARCA) on 'Policies for Balanced Economic Development in an Integrated Community' proposes an argument that is of the first importance for sustaining a socialist reality in the process of integration. The argument is based on the fact that, even under the influence of the most extreme monetarist doctrine, nation state governments have had to balance monetary measures with fiscal measures. This is because, while monetary measures — controlling the money supply and freeing prices and exchange rates — may provide an economic discipline to check inflation and eradicate inefficiency, they do not in themselves ensure economic activity at optimum levels. Those groups and regions endowed with rich resources, skills and equipment that meet current demands will survive and prosper. Others less well placed on poor, exhausted or contaminated lands, and in industries for which demand has declined, will languish and die. And their failing purchasing power will pull down the growth elsewhere. The unregulated market has always led to uneven development. Only the fiscal policies of national governments have, by redistributing incomes to disadvantaged groups, succeeded in sustaining economic growth.

The proposals for European Economic and Monetary Union and for a single market by 1992 can provide the discipline which will relate growth of income to productivity and wipe out inefficient producers. These proposals need to be balanced by fiscal measures to relax taxation and increase spending for groups and regions which have fallen behind, and will suffer from the new discipline of competition. But, in the process of integration, national governments' fiscal as well as monetary powers will be increasingly limited. The obvious need is for European fiscal measures to balance the monetary measures. The budget of the European Community is already designed to redistribute incomes — but only to one group, the farming community. The budget, moreover, is very small — only just over 1% of the combined GDP's of the twelve countries — compared with the 40-50% which national governments deploy, with transfers to poorer regions in some cases (e.g. Italy) amounting to 25-30% of GDP. Of the Community's 1%, the greatest part is consumed by the Common Agricultural Fund. The Social Funds are quite inadequate for correcting the regional disparities in productivity which now exist, let alone those which will emerge in a single market. The integration of Eastern Germany into the Federal Republic has shown just how much redistribution, including reinvestment and retraining, is involved in correcting such disparities. And these calls on European funds will come at a time when the demands for common measures of environmental protection, energy saving, and new forms of transportation are becoming unavoidable.

Parliamentary control

The ARCA paper argues that the corollary of an expanded Community budget is not only some reduction in nation state central budgets, with more funds going to local authorities, but equally for an expanded role for the European Parliament in the budget making procedure. Open debate on budgetary allocations will alone, in a centralised monetary system, give the chance to press their common cause to the groups and regions which are being held back by restrictive financial policies, such as the richer members with their stronger currencies will tend to prefer. Bankers in charge of monetary measures will not only have to be made accountable to popular review, but should on no account control fiscal policies. These will need to include deficit financing for counter action in cyclical down-turns of the world economy, as well as borrowing for investment programmes.

The Commissions's Basic Document on Economic and Monetary Union, when it comes to proposing a treaty to establish a new Community monetary institution to be called the European System of Central Banks (ESCB) or EuroFed, lays down three fundamental principles:

"— the objectives: price stability. Subject to this objective, the EuroFed should support the general economic policy set at the Community level by the competent bodies;

— independence of EuroFed from national governments and Community authorities;

— democratic accountability".

In respect of the last principle the document states that

"— the European Parliament would be consulted on the nomination of the President of EuroFed, the definition of multi-annual guidelines, the granting of special financial support, and on the recommendations. . . . it would regularly debate the Community's economic and monetary policy, with a general debate held once a year during which it would *give a discharge to the Commission in respect of its economic policy responsibilities . . ."* (emphasis added).

To this, the European Parliament in its Interim Report on Economic and Monetary Union of April 1990 responded by insisting that the "European central banking system should be created that decides autonomously how to implement the monetary policy agreed by the Council and approved by the European Parliament, while ensuring price stability and supporting the objectives of *the general economic policy formulated by the Council and the European Parliament"* (emphasis added).

A larger budget

In this Interim Report, the Parliament in fact put forward a whole series of recommendations in its motion for a resolution to the Commission, the Council, the governments and Parliaments of the Member States, all designed for "strengthening the role of the Community budget with a view to promoting the social and economic cohesion of the Member States." The Commission in its Basic Document, while declaring its total commitment to price stability, sound finance, and the elimination of high budget deficits, had recognised the existence of regional disparities. But it took a highly optimistic view. "The currently less well-off regions", it declared, "have a real opportunity for rapid catch-up, if they maximise potential synergies between EC policies (in particularly structural ones) with national development efforts. Economic and monetary union, like 1992, is a positive sum game." In other words, the rising tide will raise all boats, but what if some are leaky? "In the light of experience structural and regional policies will have to be evaluated and if necessary be adapted and strengthened."

The Basic Document speaks of "specific Treaty provisions providing a unified legal basis for Community action, in particular with respect to highways and railways, telecommunications and energy distribution networks . . ." and "encouraging the adoption by labour markets of the best observed practices for labour market management . . . concern(ing) especially mobility, permanent education, training systems, the introduction of new technologies,

and efficient methods of collective bargaining . . . to give substance
to the Social Charter . . . "But the document is extremely coy about
funds for all this. Only for the final stage of economic and monetary
union are "the following specific co-operation instruments
proposed:
— plural-annual economic policy guidelines
— reinforced multilateral surveillance of economic policy,
including rules for budget deficits
— a special financial support scheme."

"An extension of Community financial activity would have two
dimensions: an extension of the volume of budgetary expenditure
and of loans and a more flexible use of financial means." But the
Commission insists that "such a gradual increase would not imply
a large-scale transfer of major expenditure responsibilities from the
national to the Community level . . ."

By contrast, the European Parliament's Interim Report is far more
robust;

"Economic and Monetary Union", it considers, "cannot be
regarded as a realistic prospect unless at the same time the
Community provides itself with the legal, budgetary and institutional
means of ensuring greater co-ordination and convergence between
the Member States' respective economic policies with a view to
greater economic and social cohesion within the Community."

"(It) cannot imagine", so it goes on , "that such a system would
work unless budgetary policies are closely co-ordinated to ensure
that they are consistent with a monetary policy aimed at promoting
stability and with other policies geared towards various *other
objectives such as balanced growth, full employment and a clean
environment*" (emphasis added).

A greatly expanded European budget should enable the financing
of European-wide infrastructural development in communications,
transport, energy conservation and ecological protection, and also
for aid under the Lomé Convention, which have always been
stronger in the rhetoric than in the reality of Community
pronouncements.

A single currency
There is one respect in which the ARCA paper's recommendations
should be queried. This is in regard to its rejection of monetary
unification. This is said to be on the grounds of the costs and other
problems involved in such an operation, which presumably refers
to the effect on national pride of not having 'one's own money'. It
is assumed that the present sophistication of foreign exchange
markets can limit the risks and costs of continuing exchange

fluctuations inside the monetary union. The arguments in favour of having a single currency are, however, very strong.

First, there must be some economies of scale in printing and minting one set of notes and coins instead of twelve.

Second, the costs of running the exchange markets themselves, as well as of all the banks and offices where money is changed by travellers, are very large, and considerable savings would follow in all of these.

Third, it is inevitable that with 12 separate currencies there must, even within the fixed limits of a monetary system, be fluctuations which tend to exaggerate temporary movements of supply and demand between currencies, especially in the leads and lags of transfers inside transnationally operating companies.

Fourth, and most important, is the clarity of comparison for all to see that must emerge between the wages and taxes, the benefits and other social provisions in each of the twelve states, when all can be expressed in the same currency without the obfuscations of varying exchange rates.

Fifth, and following from the fourth, while at first the transition to the ecu will be popularly held to be the cause of rising prices where entry into the EMS involves a currency devaluation, in the long run the value of the Social Charter can only become apparent when social provisions everywhere are made easily comparable.

One of the major advantages to be gained from European economic and monetary union will be the role which a unified Community, with its preponderance in world trade, could play in bringing a new order into international economic relations. Once more, monetary measures of discipline, as they are applied internationally through the International Monetary Fund, have been shown in relation to the developing countries and regions to be wholly inadequate without corresponding measures of support, to offset the uneven development and subsequent grotesquely unequal distribution of wealth. In this respect also, the ARCA paper needs to take the argument further.

Towards a world money

The fact that there will be three major currencies in the world — dollar, yen and ecu — does not at all ensure that they will be constructively used. When there was only one world money — the dollar and before that the pound sterling — world-wide economic development was generally ensured by large outflows of investment backed by gold from the centres of accumulation. The reverse flow of funds currently moving *from* the developing *to* the developed countries as a result of debt repayments is beginning to work back in falling orders by the developing for goods from the developed. The actual decline of many African economies — so-called 'negative growth' — which were once a market for European producers (accounting for 60% of Africa's industrial imports) means depressed European exports.

Nothing that the Lomé Conventions have done has served to raise the African, Caribbean and Pacific (ACP) countries' share of European Community imports; and the single market by 1992 is set to undermine what protection the national member states have been able to give to their ex-colonies. The 'structural adjustment', which is recommended now to developing countries in the face of falling commodity prices, cannot take place without funds from outside for capital investment and the opening up of markets now closed by protectionist policies such as the Common Agricultural Policy. If regional aid for industrial development and infrastructural improvements were to be provided for areas of economic decline including old farming areas, this could replace the present agricultural subsides and end the damage done to Third World producers.

Moves to balance monetary union with fiscal measures, which the ARCA paper recommends, are thus very much to be welcomed in the development of both internal and external economic policies of the European Community. A strong role for the ecu both inside and outside the Community is a desirable objective, but it will not be enough to build a new economic order or even to prevent the collapse of the present order. At the present stage of human development, it is not possible to envisage fiscal policies of income resdistribution on a world scale. But something can be done, apart from reversing the declining handouts of aid, to generate world development on a sustainable basis. For that, we shall have to return to the Keynesian prescriptions for an earlier era when there was no single dominant economy and ruling currency.

Keynes's Bretton Woods design was for genuinely international institutions with a world money, not dominated by any one. To build a new economic order for the whole world, and not just for the rich minority, the controllers of the three major currencies today, with their gold and hard currency reserves, will need to make room for other currencies backed by mineral and raw material reserves, as was recommended by Professors Hart, Kaldor and Tinbergen at the first United Nations Conference on Trade and Development (UNCTAD) meeting.

It is not merely common justice, or even the narrowness of a base for world economic development which excludes three-quarters of the people, but the urgent necessity to conserve the non-renewable resources of the earth — in the land, sea and air — that dictates the establishment of a world money, in which everybody has a proper share. Only an integrated Europe could be expected to have the political will and the economic power to bring this about, together with the necessary associated measures of trade development, in the way that Keynes envisaged an International Trade Organisation at the centre of international financial institutions built upon an international currency.

All this may appear to some to be a diversion from the urgent tasks of European integration and from satisfying the claims of Northern and Eastern Europe to a place in the 'European Home'. These measure to open European markets to the Third World will, however, have to be tackled unless the European Community is to become a fortress surrounded by protective walls, not just against the competition of the United States and Japan, but against violence and disorder among the poorer two-thirds of the world's people suffering from a decline in living standards while their resources are extracted for use elsewhere by the richer third of the people. Even if it were morally defensible, such fortress building could hardly survive in a world which has only one atmosphere and one eco-system. The Gulf War serves as a terrible warning.

References

"Policies for Balanced Development in an Integrated Community" was submitted by the Association for Applied Research in the European Community to the socialist group of the European Parliament in April 1990.

The Basic Document of the European Commission for the Inter Governmental Conference on Economic and Monetary Union was published by *Europe* Press Agency No.1650/1651 of 27 September 1990.

The Motion for a Resolution of the European Parliament on Economic and Monetary Union was published as Session Document A 3-99/90 of 27 April 1990.

CHAPTER 4

A New Model of a Democratic Market

Plan and market

In the analysis of political economy, a false dichotomy has often been made between plan and market — the plan being assumed to be an all embracing set of commands in a centralised authoritarian state, and the market a set of free exchanges unregulated by authority. The collapse of the command economies of the Soviet Union and East Europe has led to a compounding of the error. Both sides presented the arms race as a struggle between two systems. But the defeat of the USSR in this race had more to do with the failure of a less developed economy to compete with a more developed as the stakes were raised, than with the difference in systems. There is widespread planning of an authoritarian kind by both military commands and giant companies in the West; yet it is asserted that planning has failed, and the only alternative is the free market. In fact, there is no need for planning to consist of a series of authoritarian commands, although it certainly did in the Soviet Union and East Europe; and the market has never been unregulated. The bourgeois state did indeed free the market from certain kinds of control exercised by monarchy, monopolies, landlords and bureaucrats. This is the freedom for which the blessing of Adam Smith is so regularly invoked. But Adam Smith made it very clear that this freedom had to be moderated by the force of "sympathy" which cemented the social and economic fabric of society. This, then, provided the "invisible hand", and not at all the forces of an unregulated market. The nation state had thus to impose its own controls on the market, not only to protect the private ownership of capital and the capital of its nationals against others, but, whether we attribute this to what Smith calls "the sympathetic feelings of the impartial and well-informed observer" or to pressure from working people, also to offset the tendency of free market capitalism to generate inequality and to waste resources.

For, it is accumulation of capital that is the driving force of industrial capitalism, and the means for this accumulation has been the reduction of labour costs, not only by the exploitation of labour, but by the employment of fossil fuel energy in mechanised production. In the competition between rival capitals, the size of the accumulations of capital has remorselessly grown. Only a corresponding growth in the powers of the state has served to counteract the tendency of the economy to generate increasing inequalities, first by enlarging its boundaries in federations and empires, and secondly by extending its social provision. While the role of the state in the first case is the origin of imperialism, in the second case it is the origin of the welfare state. For a time the two ran together. After the first stage of plunder in European colonies, imperial investment mainly by European settlers with state support spread wealth rather than concentrating it. At the same time, social provision widened the market inside the main centres of accumulation.

State regulation of the market

The nation state which grew up with the growth of capitalism has performed both the protectionist and the welfare function successfully enough for the industrialised economies of the First World up to the present day, but can do so no longer. This is partly because most of the 159 assorted nation states of today which emerged from the break up of empires are far too small to perform either role, and partly because even large states cannot regulate the activities of giant transnational companies, let alone protect the whole global eco-system. The superpowers have kept, or deliberately failed, to keep the peace, and the most advanced industrial economies — the United States, Germany and Japan — have set the rate of growth of labour productivity and therefore the rates of interest and of inflation. The giant transnational companies — far more powerful than most states — have set the level of taxation by granting or withholding their investment, and have thus determined the level of provision of welfare in any separate state. Nothing has mitigated the pillage of the earth's finite resources.

Adam Smith's "impartial and well-informed observer" looks in vain for the international order that could regulate the world market. Those who look to the European Community for the protection and the social provision which European nation states can no longer provide, will have to accept a common currency, but will need to insist on a common social budget and overseas aid programme. Otherwise, the unregulated market will simply result in gross inequalities, most uneven rates of development between regions, both inside and outside the Community, and no checks to environmental degradation. But there are limits to what even a large federation can do in Europe. The super-powers, as we have thought of the USA and USSR, are federations, but they have signally failed in their different ways to provide a decent living for all their citizens, or to prevent the most profligate waste of resources and the most damaging assault on the global eco-system. Some single world authority is called for to correct the inequalities in development and the quite unsustainable nature of current forms of development.

After the Second World War there was created a structure for an international economic order under the umbrella of the United Nations, but in reality this depended on the hegemony of the United States. When this was challenged by Germany and Japan, the structure such as it was collapsed. While it lasted, the outward flows of United States gold, capital and aid served to disperse the accumulation of wealth at the centre. Now there are three centres, and, while Germany and Japan finance the United States deficit, there is once again a reverse flow of funds from the Third World almost equal to that of the early years of colonial plunder. When statesmen from the First World proclaim the benefits for economic development of the "peace dividend" that could result from arms conversion, Third World spokesmen have been heard to murmur that it is the capital that they would like to have back.

The decline of the nation state
The same logic informs the issue of the social dividend. The tendency for the free market to concentrate wealth has been ameliorated by the social provisions of the welfare state. But the wealth continued to accumulate in fewer and fewer hands. The increase in the number of shareholders which the Thatcher and Reagan governments so proudly trumpeted did not increase the proportion of capital held by small holders, nor reduce at all the relentless process of merger and take-over. Indeed, the gap between the rich and the poor greatly widened, the rich becoming richer and the poor poorer. After the expansion of social provision in the 1970s had narrowed the gap under the pressure from organised labour and the new-found power of women and young people, the engines were reversed. Monetarist policies were introduced to reduce state spending, strengthen financial "discipline", and restore the declining rate of profit. Once more, after a decade of this regulation, which is presented as a deregulation, deepening poverty and the disorder that accompanies gross inequality has swung the emphasis back to the "social" market, this time in Europe on a European wide basis. This socialising of the market is designed to increase the part of capital's dividend that goes to the least advantaged sections and regions of the population. But the central dynamic of the system of

capital accumulation remains unchallenged, and outside of Europe, Japan and North America living standards are declining and starvation threatens many millions of men and women and children.

People throughout the world are asking themselves what they can do. The fact is that in the world today there is only a very narrow space in which Adam Smith's moral sentiment is able to exercise itself. There are millions of men and women who feel the need for more equitable economic relations and for sustainable development in the light of what they see all around them, and what they read of famine and poverty and war in the Third World and of the destruction of the whole natural environment. But the influence of the "impartial and well-informed observer" on the decisions of statesmen is quite inadequate to move them from narrow defence of their several national interests to take a wider view. Such an appeal to aristocratic influence was appropriate 200 years ago when Adam Smith was writing, but it has little effect in these days of mass democracies. The masses are moved by a fairly narrow sense of economic interest as mediated through television and radio. But the nation state has been able to regulate the market because it had democratic legitimacy. Democracy can be abused. Democracy means that the people will make mistakes, but also that the mistakes can be rectified. Moreover, industrial democracy was envisaged as the complement to political democracy. The vision has to be widened to embrace forms of economic democracy, if the whole complex of modern economic relations are to be regulated. And if the nation state cannot do this effectively, then wider democratic institutions will be needed.

Meanwhile, the condition of the world cries out for global solutions to the problems of debt and uneven development, of resource depletion, and environmental destruction. One is bound to ask why a wider view should fail to prevail, since national leaders are intelligent and educated people, who do not lack the information about what is happening, nor the access to the technical means for changing the present path of world development which must surely end in disaster. The explanation for this situation which is explored in this book is that we do not have an alternative model of economic development to replace the command economy and the semi-regulated market. The commands cannot just be modified, nor the market just more strictly regulated by the state. The whole search for an alternative is inhibited by the belief that the plan and the market are incompatible, and that the nation state is the only possible form of democratic regulation. The solution must lie in finding new forms of economic association which make use of the market as servant and not master, and allow for real popular participation in planning and market regulation — in effect a democratic market.

Need for an alternative model

An alternative model has to be related to the agencies available for making political, social and economic changes. The model of the command economy had its origins in the conception of an organised mass of industrial workers wresting power from their employers and formulating a central plan for their harmonious association. It became established as a military system to defend the Soviet revolution and was perpetuated by Stalin when the Communist Party became the surrogate for the working class in carrying through the first stage of industrialisation in the Soviet Union. Attempts to decentralise the over-centralised command system under a bureaucracy that had come to usurp the Party itself only led to the creation of a number of ministerial empires dominated by the military industrial complex. The great potential advantage of planning — the overall allocation of resources to avoid waste and correct inequalities — was lost in internecine struggle between ministries, modified only by corrupt practices and the hegemony of the military.

Outside the Soviet Union, the model of a command economy attracted support over a long period among industrial workers because of its apparent success in eliminating the scourge of unemployment, and because of the Red Army's real success in stopping Hitler's conquest of Europe. For the people of the Third World what was impressive was that a command economy had succeeded in the first stage of industrialisation where capitalism had failed. But the model was based on the agency of massed industrial workers. These did not exist in the Third World, and have ceased to exist in the First World, where a once homogeneous working class has become fragmented into a multitude of sectional interests — a new professional and managerial middle class, workers in offices apart from factories, skilled and unskilled, full-time and part-time, separated by race and gender and nationality into thousands, even millions, of isolated groups, which capital can divide and conquer. The new model, if it is to replace the dominating role of private capital in the market, must build upon this differentiation to find common cause through democratic means.

The unity in diversity attained through the nation state has been its chief contribution to human evolution, and the foundation of the prodigious multiplication of the human population in the last millenium. If the nation state can no longer provide the framework for diverse gifts within one spirit, it is not likely that meetings of nation state leaders will do better. They act for their states and not for their nations. The United Nations is based upon a Charter which proclaims the intentions of what "We the peoples" will do, but thereafter and in its activities it is states that are recognised and state governments that are represented. The United Nations has a certain authority in requiring the peaceful settlement of disputes, in advocating economic policies, and through the World Bank and IMF in allocating funds supposedly to correct the growth of inequalities in development. But between state governments and bank officials the voice of the people is lost. The need for a central authority to correct uneven development becomes even stronger.

The debt crisis as an example

Let us take an example of the greatest importance for many both in Eastern Europe and in the Third World, whose whole future livelihood is threatened as a result of the collapse of their economies. In both cases the cause is the same — the combination of the decline in prices of primary products in the world market and the overwhelming burden of high interest bearing debt owed to the First World, together with massive levels of military exenditure. With each year that passes that the debts are not repaid, the sums owed accumulate until they are today many times the original borrowings. To try to pay off the debts, the governments of both Second and Third World countries have sought to step up the exports of their primary products. The flood of goods onto the world market has weakened all prices for such products, deprived the people of the food which they would have eaten, laid waste the forests, and created deserts from mono-cropping where once there was self-subsistence farming. Faced by a rising tide of imports, First World governments have sought to protect their own farmers by means of subsidies and other measures of farm support, and at the same time have imposed taxes on any imported goods that are in competition with those of their own nationals. As each state raises barriers to the others, the whole level of world trade is reduced. Only those with the lowest costs — the agro-industrial producers of North America — want the barriers lowered; and this is what the United States negotiators are looking for in the current Uruguay Round of talks under the General Agreement on Tariffs and Trade (GATT). The result of this would be to ruin small farmers everywhere. In the end, as output was cut back prices might recover,but a whole generation of farmers would have been lost.

In this situation of burdensome debt and massive spending on armaments, the peoples of Eastern Europe have revolted and blame their military command economies, in part quite rightly, for their plight, and have put their faith in joining the market which seems to have done so well for their neighbours in the West. At the same time, the peoples of the South may still support their armed forces but are in revolt against the poor prices and the barred doors in that very same market. Governments of the North, in Western Europe, North America and Japan, are happy to help their giant companies to divide and conquer, drawing labour and raw materials freely from the East and the South. And, if they now feel obliged to give preferential treatment to the East in trade and aid, they are quite prepared to do so at the expense of the South. The cut back of imports from the First World by Third World countries required to balance their payments has inevitably led in its turn to the reduction of employment in the First World. One country's imports are another country's exports.

It would seem to be obvious enough that debt repayments are ruining both debtors and creditors. The governments and organisations which borrowed the money are in dire trouble, but the banks who lent the money are also in trouble. As Keynes once said, "If I owe my bank £1000, I have a problem. If I owe my bank £1 million, my bank has a problem." And the banks of the USA and the UK are owed tens of billions. To help them out and to prevent a collapse of confidence, their governments are easing the provision they are making for bad debts by allowing this provision to be set against profits for tax purposes, without their actually having to write the debt off. The government loses tax receipts and other tax payers have to make up the difference. The banks are rescued but no new funds are made available to the debtors; indeed, they still have to go on repaying on the old debt. It has been suggested earlier that, instead of the governments' foregoing taxation of the banks' profits, they could place equivalent monies in a fund to guarantee future borrowing to finance new trade development, on condition that the banks' debts were written off.

What, then, would be the motive for anyone doing this? For the banks it must look like pouring good money after bad. The countries that have defaulted in the past must be regarded as high-risk subjects in the future — even what is called 'unbankable'. Of course, there would be a state guarantee, but why should governments provide this except where they have political reasons for doing so, which means voters who will positively approve. When it comes down to the voters, their mood is one of beggar-my-neighbour and there has been a great deal of popular disillusion with the results of overseas aid payments. These have been perceived either as helping to finance exports by First World firms that, even if they were not exporting arms, were not exporting goods which Third World peoples actually needed, or as providing slush funds for the private pockets of government officials or even of government leaders like Marcos in the Philippines.

There is, nevertheless, a fairly strong aid lobby in most First World countries, but it tends to be concerned with disasters like famines and floods, earthquakes and hurricanes, or alternatively with solidarity with beleaguered liberation movements, as in Nicaragua or Eritrea or southern Africa. These humanitarian motivations are not to be despised, but they do not address the main problem of unequal development and declining world trade. The trade development fund raised from debt remissions could be used for resource conservation and measures of environmental improvement, as Susan George has proposed. This would win support from another section of the First World's population, those with environmental and conservationist concerns, and these two suggestions signpost a way forward for a solution of the debt problem and trade development.

Networks as a new model

What we are looking for is a widely acceptable means for encouraging an expansion of beneficial trade exchanges in place of their current contraction and distortion, building on all the diverse interests which men and women have today, now that the industrial working class of the First World and the peasant masses of the Third World have become fragmented. If military commands have failed and the market generates increasing inequalities, unless it is subject to wider regulation, what alternative model can we discover to democratise the market and planning? The answer suggested in the chapters which follow is contained in the principle of networking — networks that bring together groups of producers and groups of consumers which share a common interest. We have already noted the common interest of political solidarity and of ecological concern. We may extend this to town twinning, co-operative link-ups, organic farming, whole food and vegetarianism. But in the mainstream markets too, consumers could be encouraged to join together in local networks which make direct links with producers in the locality and further afield, where neither bureaucrats nor market dealers come in the way of the common interest in having real needs met when they are needed, without waste or misuse of resources and at a price which is regarded as fair. If networks on a regional and national scale were extended internationally, they would come to be regarded as the most acceptable conduits for development aid and the writing down of the debt burden. This is what the chapters which follow are designed to explore, but they begin with an examination in some depth of the forms of economic development.

If the concept of networking contains within it the germ of some new democratic structure which might grow out of the breakdown of existing international economic relations, it will require that we should abandon the mental spectacles through which we now see the world — divided between market and planned economies, and no less between First, Second and Third Worlds. The collapse of the command economies of the Second World has already made the category of a Second World obsolete, but we need to question the homogeneity of a Third World, even of a First World. We all share one world, and in it there are not only nation states, but other forms of organisation which men and women have created. The declining power of the nation state in face of transnational capital has not only demanded the formation of larger, regional federations, but has brought into much greater prominence in human perspectives, the strength of local groups and associations. We have emphasised the need to build on this diversity, but there is another lesson to be learnt. The division between First, Second and Third Worlds contained in it not just a false homogenising of rich variety, but a false division between levels of economic development based upon successive stages of technological advance assumed in the concept of development. This we shall have to question in examining where any particular national or other grouping of men and women stand in the relationship which they have to different kinds of technology, and in particular the way they look forward to making use of new technology. If there is no necessary single progression in economic development, still less is there a necessary progression through stages of technology.

On the technical and social division of labour

To propose even a multiple reticulation of networks as an alternative to the massed resources of the state, or of transnational companies, is indeed to set David up against Goliath. It also smacks of a retrospective, visionary hankering after retribalisation and the return to nature, which must seem wholly unrealistic for those who have become accustomed to electric power, electronic communications, and all the machines which now work for us. But, networking need not involve such "barefoot economics"; indeed, it can only function on the basis of the new information technology with computers and electronic communication systems. The scale of networks, even of locally based networks, need not be so small that they cannot achieve economies of scale which bring down costs to compete with the giant private companies. The range and complexity of machinery used does not become less but more, if resource conservation and ecological sustainability are to be taken into account. The new manufacturing processes including flexible automation do not, as some have suggested, in themselves create the conditions for craft revival, let alone for a decentralised socialism. They are likely to be used, and are being used, as an instrument for the centralisation of capital and the intensification of exploitation among what are now called the "peripheral" workers — women, migrants, blacks, especially in the Third World. Such processes do, nonetheless, open up possibilities for associating workers in production in ways that are not hierarchical or exploitative, but involve a major element of industrial democracy.

The key question is not about the technical division of labour — the relations in production between workers and machines. It is about the social division of labour — between mental and manual work — and the geographical division of labour — between town and country, tertiary, secondary and primary production. Just as the division between mental and manual is not the result of natural endowment but of economic structures established within class societies, whether determined by ownership of slaves, land or capital, so the division of labour in the world between the production of primary commodities and of manufactured goods, and now between both and the finance, research and development of high technology, is wholly artificial. It has no natural origin in resource endowments, but has emerged from a long history of conquest and colonial rule. The distribution and exercise of political power have altered, and the centres of economic power have shifted. But economic development remains uneven in different regions and at different levels. In the past there has been no single line of evolution, either in Marx's modes of production or in non-Marxist stages of economic growth. So, for the future, there is no single golden road, only that it should lead to an extension of popular power. This does not, however, mean that when men and women form themselves into social organisations they can arbitrarily pick and choose at will which bits of available technology they like. Economic structures have to hold together and have to be held within a formation of political economy that corresponds to their way of getting their living from the earth's resources. This is as far as we can take the Marxian view that economic conditions determine historical development. "Men make their history themselves," so Engels insisted, "but not as yet with a definite will or according to a collective plan or even in a definitely defined, given society. Their efforts clash, and for that very reason all such societies are governed by necessity . . . ultimately economic necessity." Such necessity is not only the need to get a living, but the need to survive in competition with others having greater or lesser power, whether economic, political or military.

References

Adam Smith, *Theory of Moral Sentiments*, 1759, Henry Bohn *The Wealth of Nations*, 1776 (Methuen ed. 1983).

P. Corrigan & D. Sayers, *the Great Arch: English State Formation as Cultural Revolution*, Blackwell, 1985.

Robin Murray, *Multinational Corporations and Nation States*, Spokesman, 1975.

Abel Aganbegyan, *The Challenge: The Economics of Perestroika*, Hutchinson, 1988.

Ken Coates, *Think Globally: Act Locally*, Spokesman, 1988.

Susan George, *A Fate Worse than Debt*, Penguin, 1988.

Paul Ekins, *The Living Economy: A New Economics in the Making*, Routledge, 1986.

Mike Best, *The New Competition: Institutions of Industrial Restructuring*, Polity Press, 1990.

Anna Pollert, "Dismantling Flexibility", *Capital and Class*, Spring 1988.

Frederick Engels, "Letter to H. Starkenburg, January 25, 1894", *Karl Marx Selected Works* Vol 1., Martin Lawrence, 1933.

CHAPTER 5

Forms of Economic Development

What is economic?

To speak of an economic order, and especially of economic development, implies a generally accepted definition of what is economic and what is development. There has been some questioning in recent years of the concept of development, but until very recently most people would have said that there is no question about what is economic. Originally, the word meant simply housekeeping and frugal behaviour in a household. This was extended to city states, and economy came to be associated with the structure of a nation state and studies were made of political economy. Finally, the political epithet was dropped in the attempt to distinguish means which could be described as economic and ends which were said to be political. The means were assumed to consist of a number of rational choices about the best uses of land and labour and capital. But, when the end came to be generally accepted as the growth of national output, it did not seem to be too far from the original meaning to speak of nation states *being* economies rather than *having* economies. The recent questioning of the rationality of economic choices puts all this back into the realm of uncertainty.

It gets us nowhere to say that the agreed end of economic activity is economic growth, if we have not yet decided what is economic. If it is said to be those choices which lead to growth, we are in a circle because we need to know the answer to the question: "growth of what?" The answer generally given is that it is growth of national income or GDP (gross domestic product). We shall consider in a moment some problems about measuring the size and distribution of incomes, but there is a prior question. What does national income measure? The superficial answer is that it measures the value of certain goods and services, calculated in money terms, often divided by a country's population in order to show income per head. Growth, therefore, is the increase of those goods and services. Economic choices are rational in so far as they provide such an increase, but growth may involve bads as well as goods, disservices as well as services. Economic rationality suggests that these will be avoided or at least offset. Unfortunately, as we have come to learn in recent years, almost all our goods and services have entailed bads and disservices, like acid rain, leukaemia in the blood of nuclear power station workers, and the depletion of non-renewable resources, the cost of which had not been entered into the economic calculation. Even more seriously, we have been discovering that the freedom, imagination, creativity, and even the health and safety of many men and women are still being everywhere impaired because there is no way of entering into the economic calculus these bads and disservices which arise in the processes and conditions of work.

Some critics of economic reason like André Gorz, building upon the analysis of Karl Marx, have gone so far as to suggest that all industrialisation is *necessarily* based upon the separation of the worker from the means of production, with the aim of economising in the use of labour so as to obtain a surplus for the growth of capital and thus of the economy. Since this separation causes the alienation of the worker, it has to be concluded that only a small fraction of the work force has ever benefited from industrialisation. This follows inevitably if we take into account the tests which Gorz applies — of freedom from alienation in industrial economic activity, viz. organisation of work by the worker himself/herself, free pursuit by the worker of a self-appointed aim, and personal or social fulfilment for the worker in the performance of the work. These may seem to be rather strict tests; and very large numbers of workers everywhere have chosen and continue to choose *not* to insist on them, so long as the goods and services — houses, cars, TVs, fridges, washing machines, electricity, piped water and drainage, air travel for holidays, etc. — can be obtained from work in industry. The fact that fewer and fewer workers in modern industry enjoy any freedom from alienation has been balanced against the fact that more and more can enjoy the goodies.

Two-thirds of the world's people enjoy none of these goodies, and have often suffered from the affluent one-third's enjoyment of them. But, such is the power of attraction of the image of the "good life" as presented on the media and witnessed in tourist resorts and elsewhere, that nearly all people everywhere thirst to join the affluent few, at whatever expense in alienation and even in suffering for themselves and future generations. It is not for those who already enjoy affluence to warn them off, but a society seeking to enter upon the path of economic development needs to consider seriously what its people truly want. We do not need to accept Gorz's argument that industrialisation must necessarily involve alienation for the majority of the people and destruction of nature, only that it nearly always has done so. Industrial technology *can* be used to free rather than to enslave, but probably *not* most of the technology that is on offer from the First World to the Third or the Second at the present time. For, technology is not neutral. It has mainly been developed and designed in circumstances where the return to capital holds sway over the return to labour (or to nature), and forms of technology which have been developed in such circumstances are not easily adapted to meet other requirements. Radical alterations, and even wholly different techniques, may be needed to avoid the alienation of workers and the destruction of nature in the process of economic development. But, these will not generally be on offer from those who have already followed the several existing paths of development, and may hope to profit by selling their know-how. We shall need to look at these paths in detail, but it does not seem that any of them has succeeded in avoiding human alienation and natural devastation. Are these, perhaps, necessary corollaries of all forms of development — a necessary stage that has to be passed through on the way to a higher stage of human fulfilment and natural balance?

If, in the transition to a better life, there is a necessary stage, an economic period in which there operated what the 1920s Soviet economist Preobrezhensky called "the iron heel of primitive accumulation", then it might be tolerated. But, we shall have to note, as we dig deeper and deeper into what actually happens in economic development, that the transition lasts a long time and does not in itself guarantee that the goal of development is necessarily an improvement in the condition of most men and women involved, over the lack of development or underdevelopment, as it is called, which preceded it. What, then, is it that is being developed, and what is the end result that is being sought by all the world's people, and not solely by those in the Third World or for that matter in the previously Communist-led Second World of the Soviet Union and Eastern Europe?

What is being developed?

The idea of economic development implies at once some kind of progression — from economically less developed to more developed, from economically underdeveloped to (perhaps) overdeveloped, with economically "developing" in between. It is assumed that there is a common understanding of what is economic, but we have just seen that this is far from unambiguous. It is even less certain what it is that is being developed. Is it the land and natural resources that are being cultivated, or the relations between human beings that are becoming more complex, or their ways of living and getting a living that are becoming easier and more pleasant? We have just noted that, while we used to speak of society *having* an economy, we now speak of society as *being* an economy. This means that what is being developed is not something in society but the whole of a society, or at least one aspect of a whole society. By reducing societies to economies, and neglecting all cultural differences, it becomes possible to compare societies and put them in an order of development, which can be measured. It is possible to measure income per head in money terms from all the goods and services available to the population. This, as we have seen, is the most generally acceptable definition of economic growth — an increase in the money values of goods and services in a national economy, the so-called Gross National Product (GNP), after allowing for price increases and population growth. There are considerable problems involved in giving a monetary value to what subsistence farmers produce mainly for direct consumption in their households. Yet such people make up at least half of the world's population and two-thirds of the Third World including China.

The figure of GNP per head is, moreover, an average. It tells us nothing about the distribution of income, about who is getting the fruits of economic growth, who is getting no benefit, and who is actually suffering from the process. The extra income may be accruing solely to a small urban elite, to traders and foreign agents, and may be coming from the production of crops or minerals for export, involving some actual loss to the subsistence farmers. The losses incurred by economic growth may involve quite severe hardship for certain groups in society. Women, for example, may have extra work to do in the money economy in addition to their major contribution to the household economy, and may have to go further to collect the wood for fuel. Miners and plantation workers may be forced off their lands to work at rates of pay and in conditions which are not only alienating but infringe basic human rights.

Alternative measures have been devised to obtain a wider standard of development than growth of money income. One of these is a so-called measure of the "quality of life", calculated according to average longevity, reduced infant mortality, adult literacy, numbers of doctors and teachers, and proportion of children in full-time education at different ages, etc. But such measures tell us only a little about human happiness and self fulfilment and nothing at all about alienation at work, let alone about what is naturally sustainable in the future. For these reasons, the idea of sustainable development has entered our thinking about economic development, and it is proposed that measures should be used which calculate the depletion of natural resources, especially of fossil fuels, and the pollution or destruction of the environment. And taking account of these calculations may add greatly to our understanding of development.

Even before we began to get worried about the effects on the whole eco-system of our planet earth which were resulting from economic development, a question had been raised about the idea of an unilinear form of development for all societies. Some critics even went so far as to suggest that the whole concept of development was a gigantic confidence trick played by those who regarded themselves as being the most developed so as to enable them to profit from exporting their techniques of development in exchange for the products of less developed economic activities. The question was raised whether all the economic development which has taken place since the Industrial Revolution in Europe and North America, and then in Japan and elsewhere, has been of any real benefit to human beings, let alone to the eco-system, encouraging us all to thirst more after the possession of things than the cultivation of virtue. The argument in this extreme form comes well from those who have retired to a simple monastic life. It comes less well from those who jet around the universities of the world to give lectures about this message. But it is an argument that has to be faced.

Most people in the world, and especially those living in countries which have the least developed economies, are simply not prepared to reject all that has been achieved in the economic development of the most favoured countries over the last 250 years. Whatever the deleterious effects, and many of these we know to be unnecessary, there can be no doubt that for millions of people in the affluent First World life is easier today, more fulfilling, with less onerous toil and physical discomfort, and much increased mobility and opportunity for wider experience. To say that the gain has been at the expense of the alienation of many, even in the affluent world, and increased misery and discomfort for many more millions of others among the less affluent, and of the most serious threats to the planet's ecological balance, is only a half truth. The benefits could have been more equally spread and the costs avoided both to human beings and to the eco-system. The development process has been extremely uneven. But for these reasons to argue for the total rejection of such development is quite illogical. It is evidently necessary to distinguish carefully between those forms of development which carry general benefits and those which entail corresponding heavy costs.

What is in effect being criticised in economic development for the Third World or the Second is the copying of some of the least universally beneficial and most divisive forms of development by those who have sought to follow the first developers. There is an almost religious belief among some that this is a necessary progress, that trade follows not only the flag but the mission of the true church. The Christian religion, which has been adopted chiefly by Europeans, teaches them to "multiply and replenish the earth and subdue it" (Islam taught other peoples a scarcely less expansive creed) and it is equally true that the capitalist form of development in Europe, North America and Japan carried with it a built-in dynamic for its missionaries to accumulate riches and to destroy the natural environment, including the heathen who stood in their way. No doubt, most Europeans believed that they were spreading what they held to be more civilised and more humane practices and precepts which were in the general interest. Despite the evidence of the slave trade, there was not a white conspiracy to destroy people of other colours. It was just highly profitable for some to do so. This is not to condone the worst practices of European colonialism, but to suggest that the application of labour-saving techniques, which were central to the industrial revolution (and rendered slavery archaic), and the subsequent development of industrial technology, was not itself either a wicked conspiracy or an unmitigated disaster. It can be said that wage slavery replaced slavery pure and simple. Alienation remained and was intensified for some. But, for many there were real new opportunities which opened up.

Economic resources and economic relations

From the argument in this chapter so far, the conclusion for countries and regions which have not yet been touched, or only a little touched, by the processes of economic development, is that they should not, even despite the many unhappy experiences of past development, decide to have nothing to do with it. There are possible alternative forms of development, and choosing the right one for any particular society is an important matter. No country starts from a *tabula rasa* in embarking upon economic development — not even one in which the people have liberated themselves from oppression in a long armed struggle. Most of the political and economic institutions of colonial or alien rulers or of feudal lords may have been destroyed. Key social structures like ownership of the land and of industrial and commercial enterprises may have been revolutionised. But certain basic factors remain in the products which the land can bear, with or without irrigation works, in the mines and mineral deposits, and in the productive plants that are not destroyed, the ports and harbour installations, the road and railway system and telecommunications. There are the houses that people live in, and any barns and storage places they may have, the public buildings used for schools, hospitals, offices, churches. But even more basic are the expectations of the people.

It must be a major decision for any people entering upon the road of economic development, how soon and in what way the benefits are to be distributed. But distribution of benefits — of income and wealth — as well as of costs — hardship and damage to health — cannot be determined separately from the determinants of the economic relations of people in production, which the development process is to involve. Historically, most economic development has involved economic relations which are characterised by private ownership of the means of production, and by a concentration of ownership into a very few hands, and by alienation for the vast majority of workers. This is the essence of the capitalist dynamic, and there is no doubt that it has created massive productive forces in a very short period of time. Such economic relations have, however, very obvious effects on the distribution of income and wealth, and of hardship and suffering in the process.

One of the main reasons for the rapid growth of productive forces under capitalism lies precisely in the unevenness of its development. It builds on those people who already have appropriate skills and in those regions which have rich resources. Other people and other regions are left behind. A more egalitarian approach, pulling all peoples and all regions up together, would inevitably be slower and would be frustrating for those with higher skills and better resources. They would tend to feel that they were being held back and would for that reason lack the necessary motivation to increase their production. This was the dilemma that faced the Maoist policy in China of helping all regions equally, of pooling output in the communes, and of spreading industry on a small scale everywhere. Food production failed to keep up with population growth, too much agricultural land was occupied with industrial development, and industrial growth failed to meet the expectations of the people. When farmers with more skills and better land were allowed to benefit themselves from their extra output, and when factory managers and their workers were allowed to keep more of their profits, food production and industrial output soared. It has to be added that this would not have been possible without the heroic communal efforts of the "mass line" in repairing irrigation works and river embankments, rebuilding bridges, railway lines and roads, which preceded the post-Mao reforms.

This story from China reveals at least one of the problems that has had to be faced in adopting any of the alternative forms of economic development which have been attempted in place of the prevailing capitalist form. This alternative has involved economic relations which are characterised by social ownership of the means of production. There is no doubt that in the case of the Soviet Union and Eastern Europe, where economic development took this form, extremely rapid expansion of productive capacity was achieved, and a much more even distribution of the benefits than under the capitalist form. But it must be noted that there was no difference in the form of development in relation to the aim of economic growth and the means of industrialisation, nor any difference in the results in human alienation and natural destruction. The recent collapse of these economies, and the desire of their people to take the road of capitalist development, bear witness to a most profound dissatisfaction with the results of development through social ownership. We shall examine the Chinese and Soviet alternative paths of development in detail below, but it would be wrong to assume on the basis of these particular failures that development through social ownership is impossible. Still less should we assume that all forms of development are necessarily alienating and destructive of nature. We have to look more closely at the actual means which have been employed in the process of economic development.

On ways of increasing productivity

An ideal form of development would be one where a good living was achieved, humanly fulfiling and pleasing for all, without alienation of the workers or harm to others or to the environment, and one which could be sustained for future generations. It is not helpful to idealise certain societies of the past and to suggest that before the arrival of the European invaders and capitalist exploitation all was happy and peaceful in the garden of Eden. Any study of the history of Asiatic, slave or feudal societies prior to the advance of European capitalism will reveal conditions of human misery, exploitation, oppression and violence which can rival anything which is to be found in the world today. There is a great deal of romantic nonsense written by outsiders who see only the surface and glorify the simple, unalienated work of peasant households and of primitive peoples. The reality generally includes a cruel landlord and rapacious money lender, vicious family feuds and battles over land and property and unremitting and burdensome toil, with plague and famine and the devastation of warring armies the accepted accompaniment of a normally brief life span.

The foundation of all forms of development is an increase in the amount or the ease of production of the necessities of living, which each person achieves at work in a given time. Such increases can result from methods of co-operation between individuals in production, which either ease or augment the output by more than the addition of each individual's efforts. Examples are the casting of fishing nets, hunting wild animals, constructing irrigation works, or gathering a harvest when time is limited. Such co-operation may have to go beyond the members of a family in an extended household to include village activity and even wider co-operation. From time immemorial, such forms of co-operation have existed among all the peoples on the earth. Most increases in the output of production or in the ease of production arise from the application of animal power, and more recently of mechanical energy to human muscles. The progression from the digging stick and hoe to the hand plough and oxen or horse power, to the tractor using fossil fuel energy is well known, but still not widely spread throughout the Third World. Extended irrigation, new types of seed, and the use of artificial fertiliser and herbicides have further increased the output per person, as well as output per acre. Improved temperature control and storage facilities, and new ways of preserving the produce of the land through refrigeration, vacuum packing, and so on, and the use of pesticides and other disease control methods, have greatly reduced the losses of perishable products and thus increased usable and saleable output.

There are some big question marks, however, hanging over many of these last aids to increased productivity. Tractors, artificial fertilisers, herbicides and pesticides, and temperature control systems and packaging all use up non-renewable resources of energy fuels, even if hydro-electric power is employed. Worse still, they cause serious pollution of the air and rivers and seas, and in the case of dams for hydro-electricity generation, the destruction of whole local habitats. As the fossil fuels run out, and pollution control measures become more costly, the price of these aids to human productivity is bound to rise. What is more serious, the application to the land of more water, new types of seed, and artificial fertiliser has been found to yield decreasing returns. More and more fertiliser and pesticide have to be applied just to maintain the existing yields per acre. Increased irrigation leaves the salts on the soil, the narrow range of new seed types results in reduced immunity to disease and a loss of resistant genotypes. This is not to say, as some do, that all efforts at soil and seed improvement and all new irrigation work should be abandoned, rather that they must be more selectively employed. The use of tractors and pumps and other equipment requiring fossil fuels will also need to be far more selective. When we come to increasing productivity outside agriculture, in manufacturing, mining, transport and comm- unications, we are in even greater difficulties. The whole of modern society depends on electricity produced either by wasting fuels like oil and gas, by polluting coal fuel, by nature devastating hydro power or, the most dangerous of all, by nuclear fuel. We flick a switch for light and heat and power for small tools and a thousand people go to work for us, mining coal, drilling for oil, building dams, constructing power stations, erecting and maintaining transmission lines, and controlling the whole complex system. Even if they are not labouring, they are on duty, watching the controls. For some all this work is much more pleasant and less arduous than for others, and than many of the other types of work to be done. But the real problem is that we can't go on expanding the production of electricity by the present techniques. The fuels are going to run out and the earth's atmosphere is warming up and being polluted in ways that threaten human survival on the planet. There are, however, alternative sources of energy that pose little or no threat — from the winds, from the sun, from the tides and the waves — which could be harnessed, so that the depletion of scarce resources, the damage to the eco-system, and the threat to the health and safety of all life on earth can be minimised. They have not been fully explored so far for a reason that is easily understood. The winds and sun and the sea are free gifts everywhere. They cannot be possessed and worked only by those who command large resources of capital, as coal and oil and gas and uranium can be.

Any country starting on the road to economic development would do well to consider how to make best use of the free energy of wind and sun and seas. Of course, there are complicated engineering problems in the design and functioning of windmills, of solar panels, and of wave and tidal energy systems. These things cannot be constructed at low levels of modern technological development and, if they are imported from countries at higher levels of modern technology, they will need maintainance and repairs, including spare parts which imply in the users some familiarity with modern technology. Again, this is not impossible to achieve; but it is a sad fact that Africa, for example, is littered with solar panels and wind machines that no longer work, if they ever did. This is not so much a criticism of the African recipients as of the foreign donors who did not supply the necessary spare parts and tool kits and training for installation and maintenance. But it does raise questions about the kind of technology to aim at in the initiation of development.

Technological choices

It will be obvious from what has been said that the already developed countries have every reason to wish to impose their technology and their products on the less developed and developing countries. They regard their way of development as *the* road to be followed by all others. Their pressures might be hard enough to resist, but the internal pressures of those from the developing countries who have been educated and trained in the developed world are even more difficult to resist. They are the experts; they know; they have seen modern industrial technology at work and they want to transfer it all to their own countries. Why should they be second classs citizens of the world? The governments of developing countries have an almost irresistible temptation to introduce the most modern technology and they are under a double pressure to do so. How is a newly developing country to make the right choices about what to introduce of the new technology and what to reject?

It might be possible to review the several fields of use of modern technology and decide which were essential for the kind of society which a people starting on development wished to achieve. In other fields, then, modern technology could be rejected and for these alternative techniques could be selected. Where modern technology is accepted, it is possible that it might be adapted to the specific requirements of a particular society. It has already been argued that technology is not neutral; it has always been developed in and for a particular political-economic situation. Nonetheless, it is not impossible that modern technology might be adapted for a major change in a country's political economy. The division of labour between mental and manual activities need not be so rigorous as capitalist accumulation has required. The tests we noted for work that was not alienating can be applied. It will not be possible to speak about this in general terms. Each field of technology would need to be examined separately and in detail.

Let us take as an example the most central of modern technologies, the technology of information and computer control. Small scale computers have the most enormous advantage over all previous technological inventions, excepting perhaps the radio and telephone, in that they are not limited in their use to governments and giant companies. Any well-off individual or small company can own them, and as a result can communicate through electronic mail to all other computer owners in the same network. To take an example, my company needed in the past several days or even weeks to be sure that a message about trade prices and contracts had been received by an associate in a distant part of the world.

Today, the use of fax or electronic mail allows for instant communication all over the world at the cost of a local telephone call. Of course, most individuals in the Third World do not have access to telephones. But there are many organisations there which do, and they are to be found chiefly among those engaged in trade, where market information is needed immediately. If a developing country or any organisation in such a country is to enter the world market at all for its sales and purchases, then it must have access to up-to-the-minute information on world prices and be able to negotiate quickly and cheaply over prices, quantities, specifications, delivery dates and means of payment. This demands communication by modern information technology.

We can now look backwards from this single requirement to unravel the implications for the technological choices of a newly developing country in having the use of electronic mail. There is no difficulty about buying the computers, discs and modems, so long as currency can be acquired for purchases in the countries which produce them. But there is then the need for a telephone system reaching to the main centres of population. This needs to have a package switch system and connection with one of the international telecommunication satellites. Engineers who can manage such a telephone system and maintain lines in good order and make repairs, and even a range of spare parts, will have to be trained if they do not already exist. Computers as well as telephones also need a continuous and reliable source of electricity. This implies production of one of the several forms of energy which we considered earlier — from coal, oil, gas or hydro, wind, solar and wave power. Equipment for each can be obtained from developed industrial countries by expending the necessary currency. But once again their use implies the training of engineers who can run the system, producing the current, managing and maintaining its transmission and delivery at least in the main centres of population. To be effective and to retain some degree of independence, this implies for a developing country something more — viz. the capacity to manufacture certain parts of the system that may go wrong or wear out, for which a very high price may be demanded by the suppliers once the system is installed.

Indeed, some critics of technology transfer from the First to the Second or Third World would argue that the giant companies which can supply the equipment (for telephone systems, electric power generation, and other basic industry) will exercise their power in one of a number of ways to prevent any form of independent development. They can use what is virtually a monopoly position to withold technical information, to refuse to supply spare parts and replacements, and to charge very high prices unless the deal for supplying the initial equipment satisfies them. This may mean a continuing exclusive arrangement, through a franchise, sub-contract, turn-key plant, partnership or subsidiary company, which guarantees a future flow of profits back to the supplying company. Studies made of the role of transnational companies in Third World countries, however, suggest that there is a fair measure of protection for Third World negotiators in the still existing degree of competition between rival suppliers. But they may all be demanding similar exclusive arrangements. Third World dependence generally results rather from the ignorance or corruption of the Third World negotiators, or to put it more kindly, from the enthusiasm of Third World engineers for the technology of particular First World suppliers. Where a government is determined to retain its economic independence in importing modern technology, it can generally do so. The outstanding example is the Norwegian government's development of its gas and oil reserves in the North Sea, without involving the giant transnational oil companies. The government set up a state company which simply bought the services of the necessary experts and the necessary equipment. This involved developing the capacity to manufacture some parts of the equipment, in particular the oil rigs and the pipes, and to assemble, instal and maintain the pumping systems and refineries. For a developed country like Norway, with a large ship building industry, this was not difficult, but the principle could be applied in a less developed country.

Industrial development
The need to develop a manufacturing capacity for certain parts of equipment for a telephone system and electricity supply does not of course stop there. Transport will be needed for the engineers and for the equipment from the ports and local factories. With the necessary currency, vehicles can be bought in the industrially developed countries and petrol and oil from the oil producing countries. But vehicles also need repairs and maintenance, with spare parts and training for drivers and mechanics, and depots with all the necessary tools. And vehicles need roads and road making equipment, some of which will have to be imported and serviced with specialised tools. This will be true also for tractors and their accessories, and for irrigation pumps and pipes, if these are introduced to increase agricultural productivity.

With all these demands, it is necessary to consider developing an industrial base which includes at least some metal manufacture for repairs, spare parts and accessories, like irrigation pipes, vehicle trailers, and wheels for barrows and carts. Apart from electronics, there is only a quite small number of mechanical parts which cannot be manufactured with quite simple technical means. A good example is a water wheel for grinding and sawing and for electricity generation, which needs only a small package of components like ball bearings and copper wire which cannot be locally manufactured. How far the base is extended must be a decision of the government of the developing country. Evidently the smaller the base, the more dependent the country will be on outside suppliers, and the greater the need to earn foreign currency with products that can be sold abroad. In thinking about building up a manufacturing capacity there will be many other demands to respond to besides those of information technology and agriculture. Examples will include printing and paper making for newspapers and all forms of printed communication, chemicals for various household cleaning materials, for industrial and agricultural solvents and paints, for plastics production, and for some basic medicines. A textile industry and brick making and cement works will probably exist in any developing country, but on a small scale, and much larger scale operations will be needed to increase productivity. All these will require some imported equipment and expert assistance in establishing independent operations. So, where does it all stop?

The appropriate limits to the introduction of industrial technology such as will allow for independent, sustainable and environmentally sound development cannot be laid down as a set of hard and fast rules for any country. Each will differ according to the natural resources available, the size of territory, and the starting level of technical capacity. But there is absolutely no need for a small country to develop a heavy industry, especially since there is a world surplus of iron and steel producing capacity. Choices will have to be made between long-run alternatives, and each of these will involve consideration of a whole complex of technologies which fit together and cannot easily be disentangled. A fortune awaits the person — probably a woman — who first invents a basic sustainable development kit with successive sets to add on with each new stage of development. There will be no difficulty in starting the development process; the problem will be when and where to stop and to take stock and consider what is happening to people's lives and their natural habitat. It is possible that the people themselves will make that clear, but the fear must be that the whole development process will have taken hold of them and encouraged them to go on until they believe that they can stand on equal terms with their fellows in Europe and North America and Japan, whose activities they can see and hear every night on radio and TV.

It is the central question for world development whether all can enjoy the best of what modern technology offers already to those where modern technology is most advanced. Can similar prescriptions apply to all developers, even after building in every kind of protection against alienation and the destruction of nature? The way things stand, it is becoming statistically perfectly clear that as development proceeds, most of the people, in African societies for example, are actually falling back both in food production and in measurable income per head. Why? It appears to be because elite groups in these societies, who have a powerful influence on governments, have concentrated national resources on production for export at the expense of food for local consumption, with the aim of paying for imports of the whole range of modern industrial equipment. A few members of the elite benefit and can rival in their life styles any of those in the First World whom they once watched admiringly on their TV screens. At the same time, the mass of the people are poorer by any count. Must this be so? Is it in the very nature of development with modern technology that it should be so? We need to look at the alternatives.

References

J. Le Grand & S. Epstein, *Market Socialism*, Oxford 1989.

André Gorz, *Critique of Economic Rationality*, Verso 1989.

H. W. Arndt, *Economic Development: The History of an Idea*, 1987.

Henry Bernstein and others *Third Wrold Studies* Block I. "Third World and Development", Open University, 1980.

Paul Ekins (ed) *The Living Economy*, Routledge, 1986.

S.C. Dube, *Modernisation and Development — The Search for Alternative Paradigms*, Zed Books, 1988.

CHAPTER 6

The Choice of Development Models

Copying the First World has been the model of development exported throughout the Third World. But there has been an alternative attraction in the last few decades in the way the Second World of "socialist" states has developed in the Soviet Union and Eastern Europe. Sometimes, it is suggested that there is a third way, the Chinese way or the African way, an independent way, that is not aligned to either of the super-powers — United States or Soviet. Let us see what distinguishes them.

The capitalist model

The First World model of development is based upon the private ownership, not only of land and houses and small businesses, but of capital — that is money used to buy plant and equipment and set labour to work with it, to create a surplus after wages are paid accruing to the capitalist. As Marx pointed out long ago, the essential foundation of this system was to *free* workers from their land and other means of production and to *free* the land itself from feudal owners or from common property. The success of capitalist development is then attributed to the individualistic urge of private owners to "achieve", and the pressure of competition in a free market which makes them cut costs and keep improving their technical means of production. The traditional forms of household and village co-operation, which were destroyed by the individuation of workers, were replaced by organised collectivities of workers in factories and mines and other establishments. Such collectives of individual workers could then be managed by the capitalists or their agents in ways that placed in the hands of the capitalists the power to extract whatever profit they could gain in competition with their rivals. Workers might form unions to protect their skills and improve their wages, and such unions could wield real power, but they could generally be divided and conquered by the employers. It was in this collective organisation of labour that workers suffered the alienation of which we have already spoken.

Now there can be no doubt that capitalism through these means released the most enormous powers of production, and generated not only an industrial revolution but later also a scientific revolution. While the first introduced machines which could replace the arms and legs and backs of human beings at work, the second has begun to replace some of their sense organs and part of their brains. Marx was one of the first to recognise the colossal forces of production created by capitalism, but he warned that the free competition of many businesses in the market would increasingly change into the monopoly of a few giants, and that the structure of private capital ownership would become an obstacle to further progress. This has certainly begun to occur today. Machines now exist which could produce very, very much more than they are actually producing, but the inequalities which persist, and which have indeed increased between the few affluent and the many poor, have resulted in creating inadequate purchasing power for all the goods that could be produced. This is the paradox of poverty amidst plenty.

Was it a necessary part of capitalist development for such inequalities to exist? Could not capitalist motivation have been utilised but regulated by state intervention? Was not such intervention in fact the essence of the capitalist welfare state and of the measures which were devised by J.M.Keynes and others to counteract the worst effects of capitalist accumulation in generating inequalities? Uneven development, unemployment and waste could surely have been prevented in the working of the capitalist system by timely state action. The market could then be used as a means of exchange of goods and measure of supply and demand and as the determinant of prices without its being dominated by giant companies, or rendered unstable by the uncertainties of boom and slump? This is simply not what has actually happened. But we shall have to consider this possibility when we examine a third way between market and plan and see how far the advantages of the market can be obtained without allowing freedom for capitalist exploitation and its cumulative generation of inequalities.

Marx and Engels were optimistic about the unlimited resources available for capitalist development world-wide, although they were doubtful about the possibility of curbing the tendencies to inequality which would check that development. In the event, non-renewable resources, especially of fossil fuels, have been depleted at such a rate, and the destruction of the habitat has proceeded at such a pace, that it is now generally accepted that the capitalist model of development, as it has been established in that one quarter of the world which we call the First World, simply cannot physically be repeated elsewhere. It is a most embarrassing thing for First World experts to have to say, and quite unacceptable to many in the Third World. Some First World writers seek to defend themselves by complaining that Third World peoples, like those of the Second, are in too much of a hurry in their attempt to catch up with the First World, and as a result are destroying the very means of their development, partly by their population increase, and partly by the cutting down of forests and damming of rivers for irrigation and power generation, and excessive use of land for single crops for export. But this is only what the First World did in its development, and it is an outrageous complaint from those who have used up most of the resources already, and continue to use three-quarters of all the resources for a quarter of all the people, and to demand repayment of debts which necessitates the deforestation and desertification. What then of the model of development in the Second World of the Soviet Union and Eastern Europe, and the third way in China? Have they done any better?

The Soviet model of development

The attraction of the Soviet Union for Third World countries has not been so much the appeal of socialist ideology as the success of rapid industrialisation from a Third World level without capitalist exploitation and despite two major wars of intervention. No claims can possibly be made for the Soviet model of developoment that it avoided either human alienation or environmental devastation. *Anomie* in human exploitation stood revealed in widespread alcoholism and absenteeism from work. Massive pollution, nuclear accidents, and the destruction of all life in rivers and seas on a colossal scale witness to the ruthless exploitation of nature. Economists like Abel Aganbegyan, and scientists like Zhores Medvedev, have revealed the facts in frightening detail from the inside. But from the outside it appeared that here was a form of development that worked and had succeeded without gross inequalities, that is until the secrets leaked out about the miseries of the prisoners in the *gulag* and the privileges of the elite Party *nomenklatura*. In the Soviet model the original motivation to work was presumably the enthusiasm of socialist construction, especially in the newly developing urban areas, but this was followed by terror, first in the countryside and then spreading everywhere. It can be said that this was perhaps not a necessary element in the model and only the aberration of a cruel dictator. An industrial base was, after all, built, despite two invasions by German armies and an allied war against the infant Soviet state and subsequent blockade. While the recent collapse of the Soviet and East European economies demonstrates that the Soviet model of development has failed in the second stage of industrialisation — the development of mass consumer goods production — the first stage must be counted a success.

The fact has to be recognised that in the first stage of development there was little or no difference in the processes of production that were adopted in the capitalist and soviet models. Taylorism and Fordism were imported by the Soviets directly from the United States experience. Production processes were broken down into jobs which industrially unskilled and often illiterate workers from the countryside could easily learn to perform in great mass production enterprises. The only difference was that with state capital in place of private capital the scale of the enterprises could be larger and came to dwarf even the giant plants of the United States. The breaking down of the jobs on Taylorist principles in both cases resulted in widespread alienation of the work force. It is unlikely that it destroyed existing skills; agricultural skills were adapted and the most skilled workers moved up into supervisory and technical occupations. Taylorism also ensured effective management control in both the Soviet Union and the United States systems. Centralised planning by the Party bureaucrats and factory managers — the *nomenklatura* — in the Soviet Union took the place of direction by the owners of capital and the management hierarchies of the USA, Western Europe and Japan.

Much credit has always been granted to central plannning as the cause of the Soviet Union's successful industrialisation. This needs to be looked at rather closely. Centralised planning of the allocation of resources and of all the requirements of production, flowing in great detail from state ministries down to every enterprise and worker in the Soviet Union, certainly took the place of the market under capitalism. Such central planning and the structure of commands that goes with it generally, although not always, ensured continuity of production in place of the capitalist cycles of boom and slump, but it involved alternative types of waste. It was simply not possible to establish central control over the movement and prices of the 250,000 or so separate items which entered into all the processes of production. Only some 2,500 were selected for control by the several ministries within a matrix of centrally planned allocations between them. The ministries developed over time into little empires competing for resources and hoarding them to ensure their own successful achievements, with the military industrial complex having unquestioned priority. Much the same competitive hoarding took place at the level of the enterprise. To fulfil its plan and win the rewards of plan fulfilment, each enterprise had to obtain all the inputs that were needed and to dispatch the planned outputs. This led to both hoarding of materials and labour, and to a mafia of managers involved in corrupt practices in the sourcing of their inputs, and to an emphasis on quantity rather than quality, except where special prices were available through the restricted shops open only to the *nomenklatura* or through the black market. For the corollary of rationing and rigorous central controls was a thriving black market, with which the managers of state enterprises were intimately associated.

The irony of this situation is that the very role in which a central plan has always been supposed to exhibit its superiority over the market — that is in the overall allocation of public resources and their equitable distribution between regions and communities — failed in the face of the privateering of the ministerial mafia. All attempts at decentralising government only concentrated power more firmly in the hands of the mafia at a lower level, and the tentacles of the ministries spread right down into Eastern Europe through the operations of the Council for Mutual Economic Assistance (COMECON). Total resource planning has succeeded in wartime conditions, even in capitalist countries, when the aims of production are narrowed down to the one overriding requirement of winning the war, and when patriotic fervour is shared throughout the workforce. Such planning can be equally effective when the single aim is to build an industrial base and when once again patriotic, if not socialist, fervour is widespread. Overall planning cannot be carried over into the next stage of industrialisation for reasons that have become clear over time.

The first stage of industrialisation comprises chiefly an extensive process of adding new plants and factories and bringing ever more workers and resources into industry and out of agriculture. The second stage of industrialisation implies an increase in output per person, i.e. in labour productivity, in existing plants. This can no longer come simply from increasing the number of workers in large capital intensive undertakings, in place of family firms and other small-scale labour-intensive activities. This had been quite feasible where most employment had been in handicrafts, small mines, small-scale building and construction and haulage, and equally where in agricultural production for much of the year labour is underemployed. In this second stage, increasing productivity inside the plants and mines and transport systems means rationalisation of undertakings, which Soviet managements resisted, and the sacking of workers, which was unacceptable in the Soviet rhetoric of socialist ideology. Without any mass organisations independent of the Party and the state, the workers had no organised way of bargaining for reduced hours or more pay in line with productivity increases. They could only employ individual ca'canny and sit tight on their jobs. By contrast, in the capitalist economies the owners could ensure that management did what they were told and that the workforce was cut back in any plant where new machines were introduced to increase productivity. The workers' trade unions could bargain for increased wages in line with productivity increases for those still employed, and organise support for political parties to form governments which would provide dole money during unemployment and other measures of social security. The position today in the Soviet Union is that *perestroika* requires not only the destruction of the *nomenklatura* and an opening up of political pluralism, but a new attitude to work and pay by workers in their organisations.

In this second stage of industrialisation, the application of computer controlled automation has enormously increased productivity and required continual rationalisation of capital-labour relations. Two alternatives are possible. The capitalist way is for a small number of core workers to hold jobs which carry security of tenure, good pay and responsibility within hierarchical company structures. Almost a half of all workers can hope for this situation. The other half or more can expect no security, poor pay and total lack of control over their conditions of work. Nearly all women and immigrants fall into this category. Those reformers in the Soviet Union and in Eastern Europe who are calling for the return to private ownership in a competitive market can have little or no understanding of what the capitalist way entails for the less privileged part of the population. Their experience of what has been called "socialism" has been so awful that any alternative must seem to herald an improvement.

It is not impossible to imagine an alternative which was somewhat nearer to the hopes and dreams of the socialist pioneers. Such a democratic socialist alternative would involve retaining some general central control over resource allocation to ensure that persons and regions which were less well placed to benefit from economic development were not further disadvantaged. But it would leave to self-managed community enterprises, co-operatives and individuals the organisation and finance of production, distribution and exchange. With the aim of avoiding any return to private ownership of large capital, such an alternative has been argued for by leading economists in the Soviet Union like Abel Aganbegyan; but it implies the destruction of the power of the bureaucracy and a new birth of a true socialist ethos among the workers. As events are unfolding in Eastern Europe, it seems to be clear that only the re-emergence of private capitalists, which is already occurring in Hungary, can successfully challenge the bureaucracy, and that there is little enthusiasm among workers to assume the responsibilities as well as the power of self-management. In the very different circumstances of a Third World country now entering upon the path of development, this enthusiasm might still be harnessed to an alternative form of development.

A third way for the Third World?

It was once supposed that China might offer a third way of development between the capitalist market and a centralised command economy. Within a general system of planned allocation of resources from the centre, responsibility and power in every field of organisation of the economy, as well as of social life, were to be decentralised to self-managed communes in the countryside, and to district and productive organisations in the towns and cities. The attempt to build upon an ancient tradition of popular co-operation failed, partly because the central power remained arbitrary, closed to inspection and totally unaccountable. But an even more important reason was that the principle of equality in resource allocation to all decentralised bodies meant that those which were better placed — on better land, with higher skills, etc. — were given no extra reward to encourage them, so that they became disillusioned, while those which were worse placed were featherbedded by what was in effect a subsidy from the others. This imbalance might have been steadily corrected in due course, but in the meantime the demands of military defence and of a rapidly growing population outran the capacity of an increasingly alienated people to meet. When peasants and small businesses were once more given freedom to reap a personal reward for their efforts, output expanded rapidly especially in the countryside; but inequalities of course grew at the same time.

Could the Chinese third way have perhaps succeeded if the central controls had been more open and democratic? Without the massive arms budget, could a balance have been achieved between reward for skilful employment of good resources and state support for those less well placed? It is impossible to say, but in other circumstances than a total United States blockade and non-recognition, combined with the special historic relationship of China with the Soviet Union on the one hand and Japan on the other, the way of Chinese development might have been easier. There is a real problem of reconciling rapid development of production and equality in the distribution of the benefits , which is likely to recur in any society. It can be fairly well predicted that the current turn of China towards capitalist enterprise without any democratisation at the centre will lead to economic growth, but with still greater inequalities between households and regions, and in twenty years or so to disorders on the scale of the 1989 events in Beijing's Tienanmen Square.

Is there, then, an African way which might retain the traditions of village co-operation which colonial rule disrupted, and create forms of decentralised development within some central allocation of resources? There seems to be little evidence of this happening. As we noted earlier, African development has followed the path of capitalist modernisation for a small urban elite, leaving the mass of the people in the countryside less able than before to feed themselves, and more involved than ever in the production of export crops, for which the prices on the world market have been plummeting. Here and there, organisations of small scale agricultural producers have joined together in co-operatives and producer associations with the aim of achieving a proper balance between producing food for their own needs and crops for export. With help from foreign aid agencies, they have resisted desertification and deforestation, extended irrigation on small plots and increased production for themselves and for export. Agricultural experts like Dr. N. Shanmugaratnam of Oslo University argue that "it does not make sense to write off cash crops altogether because of past experience in production for export . . . it was not the production of cash crops *per se* but the social relations that governed their production and exchange that led to overexploitation and environmental degradation." Extending the social relations of small scale co-operative organisations onto a nation-wide scale requires government support. But such support has rarely been supplied by African governments, which have generally been more interested in large scale prestige schemes, financed by the World Bank, for river control, for example, combining hydro-electricity production and irrigation.

What would be a truly alternative form of development?
Is there a possibility, then, of finding an alternative form of development, different from either the market of the private capitalists or the central commands of the bureaucrats? It is clear from what has been said already that some elements of central planning are needed to allocate resources fairly between different regions and groups, and some elements of the market to provide consumer choice among competing suppliers. Is there a way of combining the two so that the power of both the state bureaucrats and of individual private suppliers is limited? This implies real

democratic accountability for the bureaucrats, and real control over the accumulation of private capital and the employment of labour. Different countries have developed different systems of democracy and some have sought to regulate employment conditions so as to control prices and to tax capitalists' profits. But the power of the modern transnational company is greater than that of most governments and, if a country's government attempts to exercise major controls over the transnationals operating in its territories, the company will probably transfer its investments elsewhere, or declare its profits in a tax haven.

The way out of these problems appears to be to have nothing to do with transnational companies and to keep national companies down to a small size. It was suggested earlier, however, that the surviving degree of competition between transnational companies does give to a determined government some opportunity of negotiating for acceptable terms and conditions for their operations. The obstacle is generally the corruption of the government's own ministers and bureaucrats. There remains a major objection to limiting all economic activities to those which can be conducted on a small scale. This is that certain operations in manufacturing, mining, refining, processing, power generation and transmission, transport and communications have to be on a fairly large scale to be efficient. This is not just a Taylorist and Fordist argument in first stage industrialisation, but one that applies very widely, even if a different path of development is followed from the Soviet one. Fortunately, there are many operations in second stage industrialisation which can now be carried out on a small scale using imported products of modern technology, as we have seen in the case of computers and information technology. There are also first stage industrialisation processes that can be operated on a relatively small scale, using modern materials and production processes only for certain key parts. Bicycles, pumps, carts, watermills and windmills were all examples where we saw that traditional agricultural and craft skills and materials can be used for nearly all of the finished product. We quoted several Indian research organisations which had developed appropriate or intermediate technology along these lines.

Any country setting out on the path of development will still need some large scale organisations in several of the fields we have mentioned, but also in distribution, including wholesaling and transport. The question is how to bring them within the control of ordinary people. I am firmly convinced that the answer lies in networking. Networks are designed to bring producer and consumer organisations together directly, instead of through either a state bureaucracy or private capitalists. People in both the towns and countryside can choose to join one or more of several networks. They pay a small subscription for joining, in order to finance a central office and staff of networkers. Each network has consumer subscribers, but also establishes links with producer organisations and market organisations both at home and abroad. The households which are members of the same network in any locality may or may not be members of a co-operative or local producers' association. But they will as a group establish their own popular democratic organisations. Through their network they can buy goods and services individually or as a group, by mail order or in local shops. Through the network also the shops and mail order firms will have links with producer organisations for different products and services. Some of these will be local, some in other parts of the country, and also in other countries. In the final chapter we shall look in more detail at how these might work.

Such networks would not be entirely dissimilar from the networks of suppliers which large retailers have established, like Marks and Spencer in the United Kingdom. But those who shop at Marks have no control over the organisation, and Marks uses their networks as conduits for channeling profit from the periphery back to the centre. Networks which were controlled by the subscribers would have the great advantage of being able to bring producers and consumers together in such a way that each can learn from the other and ensure that what is produced is what is needed, without waste or misuse of resources, or exploitation of producers or consumers. The networks would have a major educational and informational role, like the consumer associations with their guides on which to buy and how to choose organic and non-destructive products. But they would go much further than the consumer associations, since they would be placing contracts, monitoring quality, organising delivery — all the roles of middlemen, market dealers and wholesalers.

From the point of view of local producers, moreover, such networks provide a guarantee of a market for their produce (so long as their quality is right) and the opportunity of buying necessities in exchange at an acceptable price, without middlemen taking their cut in between. The fact is that millions of farmers in the Third World would and could produce more if the price for their produce and what they could buy in exchange made it worth their while. By linking directly with craftsmen and manufacturers in the towns, the whole level of exchanges could be raised. Through joining a network there would be a chance also of producers selling in the export markets; and one of the main roles of the networkers would be to provide information on quality control, standards, specifications, processing, packaging and shipping, which would serve to establish Third World producers directly in First World markets, cutting out most of the intermediaries. At present, the Third World producer gets only a few cents for what sells for several dollars in North America or Europe. Already there are non-governmental organisations in the First World which are establishing links of this sort, and the next step is to develop these on a much wider scale.

The possibilities open to a newly developing country of making use of the services of non-governmental organisations in the First World for developing their trade should not be overlooked. The process of trade development is one that has been pioneered by a number of NGOs like Oxfam, Traidcraft and Twin Trading. TWIN'S experience is that this must include desk studies of markets, prices, standards and specifications, and packaging and shipping requirements for any particular product; local studies of availabilities, storage and transport facilities; a joint development plan comprising decisions on technical design, training and investment in necessary plant and equipment for processing and packaging; a trial run, quality control, market research and sales negotiation for long term contracts. All this amounts to the establishment of a long term relationship of mutual trust between producer organisations in the Third World and alternative trade organisations in the First World. If a developing country is to succeed in establishing some economic independence in the world market it will need to find alternative partners in the First World so that it can increase its bargaining position with the giant companies that now dominate world commodity trade. Although it is still on a relatively small scale, an alternative trade network now exists. There is already in existence an International Federation for Alternative Trade, which unites some forty alternative trade organisations in twelve different First World countries, which are beginning to establish common programmes of work, and plan to strengthen their links with Third World partners.

The use of computers and electronic mail by networking organisations would make it possible for networks in different countries to join together in a network of networks, and set up a clearing house for bids and offers. Such a clearing house or clearing union would not require a large central staff for co-ordinating trade exchanges. The staff would be needed to service a large central computer and to advise on marrying the various bids and offers, so that they could be cleared. For the most part, those who use the clearing house would organise their own bilateral exchanges after responding to information on the electronic bulletin boards. But multilateral exchanges could also be arranged. These would need to be assisted by a kind of brokerage arrangement. There are a number of schemes which have been put forward at different times in United Nations circles for organising a trade and payments clearing union, and these are examined in the next chapter. All have been vetoed because they interfered with normal commercial and banking practices based on private profit. They should be given a trial now that both the World Bank and the European Community Lomé Convention funds are being directed towards grass roots activities in the Third World and away from the large scale prestige projects.

In the last chapter we began by raising some fundamental questions about the rationality of much economic decision making and about the assumed benefits of economic development. We have found that many of the questions were well founded — economic decisions both in the capitalist growth model and the Soviet model have not been rational, much of the development has been disastrous for large numbers of human beings, and for the whole eco-system of the planet. But we have not therefore abandoned all idea of easing and increasing the production of goods and services that we need in our daily lives. We have recommended a much more selective approach to the whole process of development; and this means taking all the circumstances of each country and region into account before embarking on a development programme. It means above all building on the practical strengths of the people, listening to their ideas and not trying to impose preconceived blueprints for utopia. For they will certainly fail. But rightly conceived in the minds of the people themselves, with the help of expert advice from those who are prepared to listen to the people, forms of economic development can be discovered which will succeed. And in this we have suggested that there may be a special role which non-governmental organisations can play both in the First and Third Worlds, and almost certainly in what was the Second World.

References

Rhys Jenkins, *Transnational Corporations and Uneven Development*, Methuen, 1987.
Abel Aganbegyan, *The Challenge: Economics of Perestroika*, Hutchinson, 1988.
Zhores Medvedev, *History of Soviet Agriculture*, Macmillan, 1988.
M. Barratt Brown, *Models in Political Economy*, Penguin, 1984.
Third World Information Network, *The Network*, vol.2. No.1. Networks and Vol.3 No.1 on Lomé IV.
D. Pearce, A. Markandya & E.B. Babier, *Blueprint for a Green Economy*, Earthscan, 1989 (The "Pearce Report").
World Commission on Environment & Development, *Our Common Future*, Oxford

University Press, 1987 (the "Brundtland Report").

N. Shanmugaratnam "Development and Evironment: A View from the South" in "Ungreening of the Third World" *Race & Class*, Vol.30 No.3. Jan-March 1989.

Manfred A. Max-Neef, *From the Outside Looking In: Experiences in Barefoot Economics*, Dag Hammarskjöld Foundation, Uppsala, 1982.

H. Bernstein et al (eds) *The Food Question: Profits versus People?* Earthscan, 1990.

ANNEXE
Some Questions for Decision in Development Programmes

1. Is the quality of life as important as the quantity of goods in the objectives of the development programme? If so, what measures are to be used to take account of "bads" and of "disservices" as well as of goods and services?

2. Is equality between persons and regions an important aim of the development programme? If so, how will those with higher skills and better resources be motivated to use them to the full, if they are held back to help others less well placed?

3. Is a rapid pace of development important? If this means major changes in land use, e.g. cutting down forests, building dams, siting new towns, how can the environment be protected for future generations?

4. Is national independence an important aim of the development programme? If so, how can technology be imported without incurring excessive dependence on foreign suppliers?

5. Are women to be given an equal place in society? If so, how are they to be involved in drawing up the development programme?

6. What are the main natural resources that can be developed, while preserving the interests of future generations? What conservation policies will be required?

7. What systems of landownership exist and what changes are planned? Has the effect of agricultural programmes on land ownership, including women's rights to the land, been taken account of in planning?

8. How can food growing be increased with less burdensome labour in the agricultural sector, taking particular account of the work of women? What will be the most suitable tools, animals, machines, water supplies, fertilisers, etc. and how can they best be obtained?

9. Is it intended that export crops be maintained or expanded to pay for imported fuels and/or technology? If so, how are these to be balanced against food production in the planning and the execution of the development programme?

10. Are most of the country's traditional exports of primary products? If so, how can value be added to these before export, and how can exports be diversified?

11. Is it intended to diversify the whole economy in adding value to primary products? If so, how large an industrial manufacturing base is to be built, what products should still be imported, and how should priorities be arrived at?

12. What pool of agronomic and engineering skills, technical and commercial knowledge and co-operative experience exists which can

be built on in the development programme? What educational and training institutions exist and can be expanded to increase this pool?

13. If transnational companies are already established in the country, or are linked to aid programmes, how is it intended to make use of their know-how and technology, without suffering exploitation by their pricing policies, and becoming dependent on their own specific growth path?

14. What trading and entrepreneurial skills exist among shop keepers, market dealers, traders and local capitalists? What means can be used to encourage them, without allowing them to dominate the producers in the economy?

15. What popular organisations, including women's organisations, exist at the grass roots which can be built on in shaping and executing a programme of development? What framework of support can be provided to ensure them financial credit, access to wider resources, and some measure of co-ordination that is not over-centralised and authoritarian?

16. Is a centralised planning authority envisaged for directing the development programme? If so, how will the ideas and interests of the men and women at the grass roots be represented in the decision making process?

17. Is a decentralised market structure envisaged for the economy? If so, how will the central purposes of a development programme be achieved to avoid anarchy without domination by a few large groups?

18. Is aid to be sought from developed industrial countries for the development programme? If so, what forms of joint enterprise are envisaged with international institutions or NGOs, to make the best use of them without advantaging one sector or region over others?

Note: Many of these questions could apply equally to what we have called First, Second or Third World countries.

CHAPTER 7

Networks: An Interface for Alternative Trade

In this chapter the concept of networking as an alternative to both plan and market is explored in relation to the quite small-scale alternative trade organisations. But it is my belief that the networking concept could be applied much more widely, and this possibility is discussed in the final chapter.

The need for an alternative trade system

For some years alternative trade organisations (ATOs) have been growing in numbers and activity; and in 1989 some 40 of them joined together to form the International Federation for Alternative Trade (IFAT) — a prime example of a "collective support system"*. In alternative trading these organisations commit themselves to a system of trade in which the partners seek to establish a more equal and mutually beneficial basis of exchange between First and Third World countries. In addition to finding a fairer relationship, the aim has been to find a more direct relationship between groups of producers and groups of consumers in the two worlds, and to help the producers to exercise more control over their primary products and to increase the value they add to them. At present only First World organisations are members of IFAT, but it is intended to incorporate partners from the Third World who share the principles of the Federation.

ATOs seek to establish trading partnerships with organisations in the Third World which

a) face special problems because of their poverty or oppression, because of natural disasters, and because of discrimination practised against them by boycotts and other restrictions on trade;
b) are committed to supporting the participation and needs of working people, and especially of women and of racial and social groups which suffer discrimination and exploitation.

*Author's Note. I have no authority to speak on behalf of the members of IFAT. They have not been consulted in drawing up the proposals put forward in this chapter.

Establishing a partnership may involve any or all of the following: financial aid; lines of credit; technical advice on production, processing and packaging; schemes of training; assistance with quality control; transport; marketing; and the sourcing of equipment needed for production, processing, packaging and transport. The essential nature of such partnerships includes reciprocal benefit, fair exchange, mutual respect, long-term co-operation and the avoidance of corrupt practices.

At the present time, each First World ATO member of IFAT has its own partnerships in the Third World, sometimes forged directly, sometimes through another First World ATO. The objectives which the members agreed in establishing IFAT are to encourage and make possible co-operation between ATOs and their partners in the following ways:

(i) in exchanging information about Third World needs and ways of meeting them, including joint supply and joint marketing;

(ii) in obtaining funding through credits and loans and working capital to support Third World trade development;

(iii) in campaigning for national and international policies that will assist Third World development;

(iv) in seeking to avoid duplication on the one hand and exclusivity on the other, when making agreements with Third World partners for marketing and representation;

(v) in generating consumer consciousness in the choice of products which conform with the general aims of IFAT.

What IFAT has now to develop is an interactive interface between the members and the system, bearing in mind the proposed inclusion of Third World members. Some matters, especially those involving joint campaigns, can be arranged at committee meetings and conferences. The matter that most interests the ATOs — the development of trading links including pooling of resources for joint supply, joint finance and joint marketing, and the avoidance of duplication and exclusivity — needs a different kind of interface. Commercial markets supply the normal interface for trade exchanges, whether between individuals or groups. Buyers and sellers can come together in a market to buy and sell, and in so doing establish relations of demand and supply which set a price and allocate resources according to the profit or loss arising from the transactions. ATOs have, however, specifically set their faces against total reliance on the market, because of the inequality of bargaining power in the market where the pull of money rules over the pull of people.

An alternative to the market is the interface of bureaucratic co-ordination. Supplies are allocated, production is ordered and distribution is organised from above by officials giving orders, according to a central plan. This has worked well in many countries in wartime and in early stages of industrialisation, but has proved to be less successful in the later stages of industrial development when increased cost efficiency and attention to consumer requirements become paramount. Such central co-ordination would be wholly unacceptable to ATOs as well as being exceedingly costly. What alternative is there, then, which would protect the independence of all the users and provide a framework for fair and mutually beneficial trade relations? The interface has to be interactive but actors with very different shares of economic and political power have to be guaranteed equality of treatment.

Networking as an interface

Most First World ATOs have in the past related both to each other and to Third World partners by networking. This means that they have not belonged to an association or federation, with a constitution and rules of association and lines of authority. IFAT is, therefore, a wholly new venture, and is not intended to interfere at all with the existing networks. These were deliberately designed by First World ATOs to encourage free and independent relationships in the Third World to further some or all of the individual aims of the several parties. Networks have the advantage that they enable groups and individuals to establish long-term links which still leave them free to make their own independent decisions within a mutually agreed framework of co-operation on specific issues. A network is not fixed and rigid like a corporate structure or hierarchy, but is flexible, continuous and capable of growing in many directions, making connections for many purposes, and always open to new members and new initiatives.

Networks have no controlling centre or leadership, but this does not mean that they have no centre and no initiators. They need a communication centre and they need networkers. The role of these is to move between groups — making connections, suggesting new linkages, repairing damaged ties. Their detailed networking is what holds the network together. Networkers are particularly needed at nodal points in different regions where many connections intersect, like synapses in the central nervous system of a human being. Networkers are not so much themselves organisers and managers, although they must know how to organise and manage. They are what we might call "enablers" or "facilitators", what the French would call "*animateurs*". They are in some ways like a catalyst, since they help others to make changes without themselves changing. They must be trusted by all parties and able to build up lasting relationships. Their most important role is, in fact, that of finding groups which can work together, which are not only compatible but complementary. Networks may be concerned purely with the exchange of information and of each other's publications, but they may involve developing actual exchanges of goods and services. These may take place through barter and other forms of countertrade or through the normal commercial channels.

How then are networks used as an interface in trade development? Many giant companies have created networks of suppliers which operate as separate companies, but on exclusive contract to execute orders to central designs and specifications. Such a network only *appears* to give independence to the producers; in effect, it gives no guarantee of contract renewal, does nothing to increase the value added locally and, even if it does not involve severe exploitation of labourers, ties the sub-contractor into a conduit of profit flowing back to the giant company. The networks of ATOs are, by contrast, designed to give real independence to the producers, to share risks and profits equally, and to help to overcome any quality and delivery difficulties as part of a long-term continuing relationship which is not necessarily exclusive, but can be opened up to others in the network. The only basis for such risk taking is one of total mutual trust.

A similar degree of trust must also be established by the ATO with its associated distributors — wholesalers and retailers. This is the more necessary because the ATO's sources of supply in the Third World, in co-operatives and producers' associations, fall outside the usual ambit of commercial trading, and it is only the good name of the ATO which underwrites the acceptability of the deal in the mainstream market. Of course, where the market is a specialist or solidarity market, the ATO can appeal to the good will of its customers; and many ATOs deal only in such markets; but the recent tendency is for ATOs to seek to establish links for Third World producers with the mainstream markets in the First World. ATOs may also have trading relations with First World suppliers of equipment, tools, machinery, etc., in sourcing these for their Third World partners. There is no reason why these should not also be developed on a networking basis, with co-operatives and other small suppliers, and this will certainly increase in importance in the future, but for the present it is more likely that normal market relations will obtain here.

Expanding trade networks

Most ATOs operate from a single centre, communicating directly with partners in different parts of the world, or through their own representatives in each of several regions. Such representatives may be networkers in the sense we have defined of making links without themselves being part of a line of command. But they have a responsibility, and are likely to have a first loyalty, to the organisation they represent. What should happen, then, when ATOs wish to work together more closely, as in IFAT, and seek to extend the networking principle rather than building up a co-ordinating structure? They will need to establish ground rules for their interaction. This may not be difficult in their own several exchanges of information and products. Problems arise when networking is extended to link together several centres and their associated networks for joint action.

Let us take first the exchange of information in what would be a networking of networks, and then turn to the trading of actual goods and services. Access to a central data base has to be assumed for copying existing information and for regular updating. Each ATO will have its own information bank. If this is held in machine readable form, then in order to combine these, there are three or four areas where decisions will have to be made by subscribing members:

1. Headings and sub-headings will have to be agreed among the users, and information will have to be stored under these codifications, if it is for circulation by automatic access through bulletin boards in an electronic mail network;
2. Some information will be classified as confidential or commercially sensitive. Definitions and rules for procedure will have to be agreed concerning the use of accessed information, and especially that which relates to commercial deals;
3. Not all information will be relevant to all parties. A filtering system will be needed for extracting only such information as is likely to be useful for groups in particular regions or sectors. This will require aditional codes added to the headings and sub-headings referred to in 1. above and the limitations in 3. above.
4. A small staff will be required at the office where the computer is located, responsible not only for servicing the computer, but also for making, updating and circulating on a regular basis an index or register of entries.

The kind of information which will be of value to ATOs in such an information exchange could include items under four main headings: partners, products, markets, technology, with cross references, e.g.

Partners — names, addresses, type of organisation, main activities, relationship with ATOs, stage of trade negotiations or details of agreements with reference to products, markets and technology, including future prospects;

Products — sources, specifications, quantities, availabilities, prices and trade development proposed or in progress, with cross reference to partners, markets and technology;

Markets — by country, organisation, products, with specifications, quantities, openings, prices;

Technology — established or on trial, by country and product, for production, processing, packaging, transport, with specifications and costings;

Just to make such a preliminary list emphasises the need for the system of classification outlined in 2. above. Where information is confidential or commercially sensitive, only the most general statements will be brought into the public domain, but even that amount should be helpful in overcoming duplication and suggesting possible lines of co-operation.

When we come to trade relations, the fact is that exchanging goods or services is more complicated than exchanging information. This is not only because much more attention has to be given to specifications in detail of quantities, quality, standards, batches, packaging, delivery dates, methods of payment, etc., if joint deals are actually to be made. It is because the essence of a trade interface is that it should be capable of being made multilateral. Deals made by individual ATOs will have consisted of bilateral relations between a single centre and its network of producers and markets. The aim of widening the network of trade exchanges implies the possibility of developing not only new bilateral deals but also multilateral exchanges. Some of the bilateral deals will have been in the form of countertrade which brought in a third party to the deal, for example, in marketing the products of a "buy-back" agreement, where all or part of the payment for plant or equipment supplied is made in the products of that plant, and these have to be sold in several different markets. The details of these deals may be of enough interest to other ATOs to circulate them in their information exchange system; but actually working them out between different potential buyers and sellers requires a special kind of interactive interface. Of course, the deals could have been been made in the normal commercial market, but it is assumed that networking has been chosen by ATOs because of some dissatisfaction among their partners with the terms and conditions which they found there. How then can a multilateral trade deal be set up through a networking interface?

Let us imagine that a Third World organisation has products available which its main ATO partner cannot deal with, or a First World ATO has a market for products which its regular partners cannot supply. Assuming that all are members of the same electronic mail network, then such offers and bids with the necessary details of quality, specifications, quantities, delivery dates, prices etc. could be posted on the E Mail bulletin boards to which all subscribers have access. This becomes a network of networks for making trade exchanges. Through it, offers and bids could be married up or new connections made by direct contact to follow up the bulletin board announcements. First come would be first served, but progress of negotiations and any breakdown in arrangements would need to be reported openly, as and when the parties agreed to do so. Such circulation of bids and offers provides a valuable extension of the trade networking of individual ATOs, but it goes no further than finding new bilateral First and Third World partnerships; and we are looking for a genuine multilateral extension of our interface in both worlds.

Multilateral deals by networking through a clearing union

Developing trade from a bilateral to a multilateral basis raises quite new problems for our interactive interface. Of course, once more there are always market channels which are widely used for multilateral exchanges through the medium of a common currency, or convertible or otherwise acceptable currency. Many organisations in the Third World, however, have no access to convertible currency, and such currency as is available to governments is pre-empted for debt repayment and for other urgent requirements. This is often why Third World non-governmental organisations come to First World ATOs in the first place, and why ATO trade often takes the form of barter or some form of countertrade, in which there is an element of non-monetary compensation. There is no reason why alternative trade should be limited for this reason to bilateral exchanges. Multilateral deals are perfectly feasible outside the normal commercial market, but they do require a new kind of interface. The possible interface which is explored in this paper is the clearing union.

A clearing union is an extension of a clearing house, which is the institution established by banks for exchanging each other's cheques, so that only the balance at agreed dates needs to be settled in cash. A union provides also for some agreement to finance deficits over a longer period. It offers a model for the kind of structure which ATOs need as an interface for multilateral trade development. Clearing unions established in the past like the now defunct European Payments Union or like the Bank for International Settlements have had government and banking support, which will not be available to ATOs, and they have been limited to clearing financial balances between states. The ATOs need a mechanism for clearing financial balances between themselves, but they need also to find a framework for positive trade development, which goes a great deal further than simply settling accounts.

It was just this which was the objective of the Clearing Union proposed in the 1960s by Dr. Andreas Goseco, a staff member of the Food and Agricultural Organisation (FAO), for consideration by the United Nations Economic Commission for Africa, and subsequently by the United Nations Economic Commission for Asia and the Far East also. It was designed as a "supplementary payments mechanism to promote trade among developing countries". A central clearing house was to be established in a sponsoring region with licensed jobbers and brokers as in a commodity exchange. Offers and orders for goods and services would be received from participating members. These would be put together and when a three-cornered, four-cornered or multilateral deal had been found to fit among participants with different offerings and different needs in different countries, they would be made up into a package of deals which were linked together as in a chain, each link depending on the one next to it. Dr Goseco took as his examples Burmese rice, Indian bicycles and jute bags, Argentine corn beef and Indonesian cocoa beans. A package of deals would be prepared and these would then be presented to each of the parties for confirmation. If the package was accepted, credit notes would be issued to each party, against which money could be borrowed in each of the several countries involved so as to finance the deals. If it was not accepted, alternative deals could be worked out.

It is important to note that these credit notes are not in themselves title to goods or services, but only a facility for obtaining title. All the legal business of transferring titles, as well as the practical business of moving, storing,insuring, monitoring of goods remains to be done by the traders concerned. The credit notes play an extremely important role in the interface of the Clearing Union. Since it would be unlikely that each element in the package would be exactly equal in value, unused credit notes, or portions of credit, could be used for further deals by those with a surplus, or could be borrowed at a rate of interest by those in deficit. Given the multilateral nature of the deals, the credit notes would in effect become money, not just as a currency for effecting the exchanges, but as an exchange reserve like gold or any hard (i.e. convertible) currency.

Dr. Goseco at the time recognised that the use of computers could replace some part of the activity of the brokers and jobbers and greatly simplify the procedure. Professor Ragnar Frisch of Oslo had already proposed the use of computers for optimising trade exchanges by encouraging nation states to submit their long term plans for trade development for reconciliation by computer so that corrections could be made in advance of either anticipated over-production or under-supply of particular goods. The size and cost of computers at that time restricted his proposal to use in planning trade between states. The reduction in computer size and cost today, combined with the development of electronic mail, have made it possible for even quite small organisations like ATOs to avail themselves of such a computerised interface.

Let us consider, then, how multilateral trade exchanges through a Clearing Union could be developed by ATOs and their partners, using personal computers, electronic mail, and one large capacity computer. Multilateral exchanges would start as a simple extension of the bilateral exchanges being made through the E-mail bulletin boards of the ATO's network of networks. Any one of the networkers operating with each of the several ATOs can spot possible third parties and even fourth parties to facilitate the trade development projects which they are enabling. The bids and offers of the several parties can be brought together on the E-mail bulletin board for discussion and negotiation; and agreements can then be drawn up for sales and purchases, each party acting freely with the full knowledge of the whole package of which his or her deal forms a part. This is important, since each deal is part of a chain and no link can fail without the whole chain collapsing. As in the Goseco proposal, credit notes would be claimed against accepted offers of goods or services, and these would be exchanged for goods or services required. Once again the credit notes would not give legal title, but would be used as a common currency for making exchanges. All the legal and practical business of trading would have to be carried out as usual by the individual ATOs. There are greater risks involved in such multilateral trading than in bilateral exchanges, but also more opportunities. Normal commercial insurance services can be used, but it will probably be necessary for the ATOs to set up a special fund to cover non-insurable trading losses incurred in arranging multilateral deals.

Here is an example. It is assumed that all the organisations involved are part of the ATOs' network of networks, but only those in the same country can make exchanges between themselves without using the Clearing Union. The organisations are for simplicity of exposition given the name of the country where they are established.

India 'A'	offers	Bicycles	wants (or will take)	Wood-working Tools
India 'B'	"	Jute Bags	"	Fishing Tackle
Nicaragua	"	Coffee Beans	"	Bicycles
Argentina	"	Corned Beef	"	Jute Bags
U.K.	"	Wood-working Tools	"	Corned Beef
Netherlands	"	Fishing Tackle	"	Coffee Beans

It can be seen that no bilateral deals are possible, but all the items which appear as "offers" appear also in the "wants" column. If the values of the various offers and wants are roughly similar, which is probably why they will have been picked out by the networkers, then exchanges can be organised by means of credit notes. Since these are in effect money, they can be used for additional purchases or sales through the Clearing Union to make up the difference in values of direct exchanges, but they can also, as in the Goseco proposal, be accumulated as a currency reserve held by each subscribing member, which can be used for future purchases without any direct exchange or as part of a future package of deals.

There remains the problem of some initial credit to start the chain of exchanges. There will be a critical number of subscribers to make such a Clearing Union work effectively, and in time it should be possible to build up a credit fund separate from the claims to credit of each member. This fund could then be drawn upon to initiate new members' deals and to cover temporary deficits. In order to launch the Union, subscribers could be expected to put in sums of money according to the use they wish to make of the clearing facilities, and this can subsequently be related to the actual turnover of business that goes through the Union. Subventions should be allowed for the least advantaged Third World producers and for newcomers from the Third World. Drawings on a credit fund would need to be subject to agreed parameters for setting interest charges or covering non-insurable losses.

It is evident that, while some of these interactions at the interface could be regulated more or less automatically by agreement in advance between the subscribers, there will be interactions which will need to be negotiated by networkers acting for partner organisations in both the First and Third World. They in their turn will need to refer to networkers at the centre for some measure of co-ordination. Such co-ordination will not consist of orders and instructions, although in the event of the Clearing Union's rules being broken, action to suspend a member subject to an appeal procedure would have to be allowed for. Normally the task of the networkers, as always in a network, would be to initiate and facilitate, but they will have some routine technical tasks. Apart from keeping the central computer working and maintaining the index and codification system, they will have the responsibility of issuing credit notes against firm promises to supply goods or services. The main task of the central group of networkers, however, will be to assist in marrying bids and offers and in effecting settlements. They will be expected to keep an eye out for possible multilateral exchanges which subscribers have missed and to help with working out deals, not only where a subscriber is in surplus, but more especially where a subscriber is in deficit. They will also have to give advice about the management of the credit fund, not only where subscribers are seriously in deficit on their trade exchanges and where there are losses to be covered, but also where flows of funds are failing to keep up with business requirements.

It is not necessary to imagine a large staff at the centre of a Clearing Union. The great advantage of the model proposed is that it is very simple. Once the system is established it becomes very largely self-activating. The subscribing groups can make use of the Union as much or as little and in whatever different ways they wish, within the general parameters of the system. There need be no danger that, as with many co-ordinating organisations, the maintenance of the structure requires more energy than is saved by its existence. There is no inherent probability, even if the staff at the centre is somewhat increased to respond to members' needs, that the Union would become like others a sort of octopus sucking the life from those held in its tentacles.

There would be no need in the type of Union proposed here for any great degree of centralisation, even among alternative trade organisations, once the principles of operation had been agreed and control of subscriptions established. From the first prototype one could imagine the emergence of regional clearing unions and of specialist unions for organic foods, to take a very pertinent example, or for vegetarians, or for those who want to be sure that what they buy is people-friendly as well as nature-friendly. This would be in line with current moves being made by a number of ATOs in Britain towards the introduction of a Fair Trade Mark, to be awarded to goods which pass certain humanitarian and ecological criteria. Extension of networking unions into the mainstream market should not be difficult, once the principle of joining a network, instead of patronising a store, comes to be recognised. The imminent arrrival of facilities for ordering goods by phone and for picking up ready packed goods of standard specifications at special collection centres will give to medium-sized distributors the chance to compete with the giant multiples who alone can afford to invest in large shopping sites, with extensive parking facilities. It is this facility which has given to mail order business its great potential, which many small distributors, including ATOs, have already taken advantage of.

Necessary conditions for establishing a Clearing Union

We may now summarise the conditions that need to be fulfilled for establishing an interactive interface for a growing number of support systems in developing alternative trade exchanges between First and Third World organisations. This could be extended. There is in fact no reason for excluding, and every reason for including, newly formed co-operatives and other producer associations, now to be found also in the Second World of the Soviet Union and East Europe, and perhaps including China, which were once marked by rigid central planning of foreign trade along with all other economic activities. The first essential condition for success is that the several support systems — in our case, alternative trade organisations — have shared aims and can agree together on common methods of work. The First World ATOs have shown this in their agreement to establish the International Federation for Alternative Trade, but they have still to incorporate Third World members, let alone Second World members. Integral to this first condition is the preparedness of all involved to share information, even on commercially sensitive matters, and to share business opportunities within agreed limits. It remains only that IFAT should make a start with a comprehensive information network and apply the experience gained in developing an interactive interface for all the support groups involved as the basis for establishing actual trade exchanges through a Clearing Union.

Given this first essential precondition of shared aims, the other conditions for establishing an interactive interface for alternative trade are largely practical — concerning finance, personnel, computer hardware and soft ware, office space, records and files, etc. — but it has to be emphasised that all these organisational matters must be subject to control by the members. The constitutional aspects of committee responsibility and personnel accountability are not the subject of this paper. Successful agreement on these is simply being assumed here, although negotiating such a framework for the interface we are proposing will not be easy and will certainly involve long and complicated discussions. The practical conditions for multilateral trading through a networking interface in a Clearing Union can now be summarised:

1. *Membership.* Members will be admitted by signing their agreement to the aims and rules of the Union and paying their subscriptions, subject to a veto exercisable by any existing Union member. The breaking of Union rules will be grounds for expulsion, subject to a procedure for external appeal;
2. *Finance.* Members will have to pay an annual subscription to cover running costs of the central office, the computer, etc. and salaries and expenses of the networkers at the centre;
3. *Credit Fund.* Members from the First World will have to contribute to a Credit Fund according to their use of the Union's facilities. Members from the Third World will only pay into the fund as part of agreements which they have with their First World partners;
4. *Personnel.* A small staff of networkers will be needed at the centre to manage the computer, to issue credit notes, and help with arranging trade deals and with managing the Credit Fund;
5. *Computer and E-Mail Network.* A large capacity computer will be needed at the centre, with its own E-Mail network, or with a link to one of the existing networks, and with an agreed indexing and information retrieval system built into the soft ware;
6. *Regional Centres.* As the Clearing Union expands its membership, it will be necessary for the facilities at the centre to be replicated in three or four main regions of activity;
7. *Accountability.* All personnel employed by the Union and all activities going through the facilities of the Union, or being exercised in the name of the Union, will need to be subject to democratic control by the membership;
8. *Corruption.* There will have to be an absolute ban on all forms of bribery and corruption, and on any concealment of information which is required under the Union's rules.

As a final conclusion, it may be remarked that a successful development of alternative trading through a Clearing Union could lead to a major challenge to the operations of the transnational corporations and of the commodity markets themselves, where the transnationals now dominate all world market exchanges. For such a challenge to be sustained, consumer consciousness of Third World needs (and equally of ecological constraints on the free market) would have to grow to a point where a really large proportion of the population in the First World chose to buy from ATOs, such that retail organisations would emerge everywhere on a large scale with links to the networks of Clearing Unions. At this point the scale of operations of even a number of regional Clearing Unions would become too great for effectiveness. A large number of such Unions linking producer organisations and consumer associations would emerge in each country, increasingly replacing the transnationals as the major traders between the First and Third World — and perhaps the Second World too. That situation would require new forms of network co-ordination which cannot be examined now, but the model of the clearing union indicated here could be applied to establishing a clearing union for clearing unions in line with a network of networks. Nothing that is here proposed, of course, eliminates the necessity for creating a new international economic order with agreed rules for resource conservation and environmental protection, but the existence of flourishing, democratically controlled international trading networks should generate new confidence in the possibilities of international cooperation, which neither the giant trans-national company nor the many separate nation states can now provide. At the same time application of the networking principle need not be restricted to international trading. It could provide the framework for new ways of linking producers and consumers inside each country, combining social responsibility in resource allocation with democratisation of the market. And these are discussed in the final chapter.

References
Andreas Goseco, *A Supplementary Payments Mechanism to Promote Trade among Developing Countries — A Proposal.* U.N.Economic Commission for Africa E/CN. 14/WP.2/2, 28 July 1985.
Ragnar Frisch, "A Multilateral Clearing Agency", *Economics of Planning*, Vol.7. No.2. Oslo 1987.
M. Barratt Brown, *Countertrade*, TWIN, 345 Goswell Road, London EC1., 1987.
Diane Elson, "Market Socialism or Sovietisation of the Market", *New Left Review*, No.172, Nov-Dec 1988.

CHAPTER 8

Agencies and Directions of Change

The socialist project has always been about the mobilisation of workers' power to establish a more just society, with more equal distribution of wealth. The great divide in the movement has been related to the way in which this power should be used — by direct assault and seizure of the centres of unequal wealth or by regulating the market in which that wealth is generated. There was a common assumption, except on the anarchist wing of the movement, that power could be applied from above to the management of society and especially of the economy, qualified by forms of democratic accountability, both economic and political. As a result, the advocates of the seizure of power, where they were successful, found themselves exercising power by increasingly authoritarian measures in command economies; while those who sought to regulate power became increasingly incorporated in the very power structures which they had set out to regulate. Socialism had ceased to be democratic. Democracy had ceased to be very social.

What power to the workers?

Were the anarchists — from Bakunin onwards — perhaps correct after all, that in the words of a liberal constitutionalist "power corrupts and absolute power corrupts absolutely"? Or, was there a fatal flaw in the assumptions made about social, and particularly economic affairs, that these could be managed from above? Workers who could seize power in the factories or on the streets — in Gdansk or in Prague — had evidently no clear view of an alternative way of organising the political economy other than to alter the leaders at the top. It has seemed necessary, therefore, to examine the actual processes by which wealth is generated and the actual links in command economies and in market economies that exist between workers as producers and as consumers, to discover agencies and directions of change. Moving beyond the unequal power in the work place, what was it that was to be managed or regulated in the economy? Marx had proposed that capitalist society was built upon the exploitation of workers who owned no means of producing a livelihood by those who owned all the means. The injustice was to be righted by seizing the means, but where this was done it did not end the inequalities in the distribution of power and wealth in society. Yet the attempts of those who rejected Marx to concentrate on regulating that distribution without correcting the basic inequality at the work place seem to have had no greater effect. Moreover, both Marx's followers and the Social Democrats have failed abysmally to conserve natural resources or protect the environment from destruction which threatens all life on earth.

The result of market regulation, at least in the advanced industrial societies, is that some of the worst aspects of inequality had been corrected. The most disadvantaged and impoverished groups had been raised from absolute privation. Some extremes of wealth had been reduced. More important than such changes at the top and bottom of society was the fact that a large middle section of the population had been raised to conditions of comfort and enjoyment of luxuries which had once been the preserve of the very rich. But, outside of the advanced industrial societies among the remaining three-quarters of the world's population, the poverty of the great majority remained unalleviated; the few rich had lost little if anything of what they had and only a tiny middle section had achieved the degree of affluence enjoyed by the majority in the advanced societies. Why had the benefits of modern industry not been spread more widely? The answer must be that the tendency for the market to perpetuate and indeed to generate inequality, since the market responds to the pull of money and not of people, had not been corrected. Only in a few societies — Japan, South Korea, Taiwan — did new centres of capital emerge to challenge the cumulative power of established wealth, and in the interests of the few who were the new accumulators. While in the societies with command economies which had escaped from market forces, power was exercised from above mainly for the benefit of those at the top. The unequal distribution of wealth and power was hardly changed, although the rhetoric had it that these were workers' states.

The question was inevitably raised both in the advanced industrial societies and in the so-called workers' states as to who were now the workers. A whole school of socialists, mainly in the United States of America, held out no expectation of social change proceeding from the affluent First World, or from the Second World of workers' states, but looked for a revolutionary seizure of power to the impoverished peoples of the Third World and their emigrant populations in the First World. These were the real workers — in the mines of Africa, the factories of Asia and the plantations of the Americas. They could point even to some small shift in manufacturing from Europe to Asia (outside of Japan) and from the north to the south inside the USA itself. While the seven main industrial capitalist countries continued to account for 75% of world manufacturing output and 64% of all world industrial production, it seemed to be asking the tail to wag the dog to expect the Third World to lead the revolt. The scenario was coloured by the expectations of rising consciousness in Africa, Asia and South and Central America against their domination by white people who were demanding repayment of money borrowed for industrialisation on a scale that was causing a massive reverse flow of funds from poor to rich. Hard won improvements in living conditions in many Third World countries were being eroded. Would the masses there but revolt and then they would find allies enough in the First World where inequalities were growing? For, while the middle section had been improving its position, the poorest third to a quarter — migrant workers, unemployed, pensioners, single parents, part-time and contract workers — had been suffering an absolute decline in living standards, at least in the United States and United Kingdom. Was this then to be the basis of the appeal for workers of the world to unite — the deprived in the First World and the dispossessed in the Third?

Who are the workers?
Of course, it would be absurd to suggest that all the full-time workers in both the First and Third Worlds — the so-called core workers — are now in the affluent middle section referred to above; but a lot of them are, especially in the more advanced industrial countries. Certainly, the workers from whom Marx and his followers expected the most committed revolutionary action in the centres of developed capitalism are much reduced in number. These were the great assemblages of workers in factories and mines and transport depots who were organised into trade unions. The socialising of production was expected to create the necessary consciousness and the necessary organisation for revolution. In fact, Marx worked most closely with leaders of the skilled trades' unions who were in the end more interested in retaining their wage differentials over their fellow workers than in fomenting revolution. Marx's International was effective to the extent that it served to unite tradesmen whose position was threatened throughout Europe by their employers' recruitment of cheap labour from the countryside. Women and blacks complain today of trade unions having changed very little in this respect.

Who are then the workers of today? In terms of Marx's definition of a worker as one who depends for his or her livelihood on going to work for someone else, there are far more workers today than in Marx's time. In the UK, although the numbers of employers and self-employed have been growing again recently, the overwhelming proportion of the population of working age — 24 millions out of 29 millions — are employees, and the two million unemployed would prefer to be employed. Only just over three million are self-employed, with or without employees. If workers are defined by occupation, then over 60% of men and 45% of women in Great Britain are classified as manual workers. There has been little change over the years in this respect; the big changes have come in the sectors of employment. In the UK again far fewer are in manufacturing — only five million compared with eight million twenty years ago — and another eight million are in primary production of food and energy and in construction. That leaves nearly 70% engaged in providing services. Most of these are women, who now make up almost half (48%) of the labour force, about 40% of them working part-time. With these changes has come a great decrease in the proportion of all employees organised in trade unions. This is now less than half of the total employed in the UK, rather under two-thirds of the men and one-third of the women. Proportions are much lower in most other European countries. Even smaller proportions of workers are organised into unions in the Third World.

Not only has there been a major shift from men to women, from full-time to part-time work and a slight shift from First to Third World, but there have been corresponding changes in the size of work place and the location of employment. The average number employed in each work place in the UK has steadily fallen over 30 years from 120 to 30, and the number in establishments of over 1000 from 35% to 18%. At the same time in the UK, while employment has risen in twenty years by a million in the South East of England and by nearly another million in the South West and East Anglia taken together, there has been no growth in the North and Midlands, in Scotland, Wales and Ireland, where unemployment rates are very much higher. These areas where organised workers were once most heavily concentrated now account for less than half the total UK labour force. Moreover, many plants are not now to be found in the big industrial cities but in small towns and in the countryside. And this picture is repeated all over Europe and in North America. Why has it happened? And what does it mean for the traditional socialist expectation that workers' power could be mobilised from the major centres of organised labour whether for the purpose of taking over the state or of regulating the market. Do these shifts, moreover, offer any new hope for correcting the massive inequalities which continue to disfigure human societies and of ending the pillage of the earth's resources and the poisoning of the environment?

It has become fashionable to pillory Marx for his predictions of increasing misery and the breakdown of the capitalist order through cumulative crises of overproduction. His critics point to the affluence of the "immiserated workers", but the facts today on a world scale of debt and starvation at one pole and of food mountains and unemployed plant and workers at the other do bear a strong resemblance to the outcome that he predicted. Yet, the workers who were to be the grave-diggers of the system, where are they? It was understandable in Marx's day to see the increasing number of men and women forced into wage labour from peasant households and self-employed workshops as an increasingly homogeneous proletariat ripe for revolution. It may be that the divisions between First and Third World, between white and black, core and periphery, men and women, full-time and part-time, skilled and unskilled, upon which the owners of capital could depend, are no greater today than they were in Marx's time. But one thing is certain. There is no longer the concentration of workers in organised echelons in the great industrial centres that there was at the end of the Nineteenth Century and even right up to the 1960s. What has happened?

The new technology
The fact is that the machines which the workers work with, in offices as well as in mines and factories, have been revolutionised. The working class of the late Nineteenth Century was employed in hierarchical structures in which manual and non-manual operatives were sharply distinguished. Mass production of identical products and parts of products was coming in the United States to be based upon the repetitive precision engineering of the Springfield Armoury and the time and motion studies of F.W.Taylor. Design and co-ordination were taken "upstairs" out of the hands of the skilled workers, whose expertise Taylor had studied. The execution of orders issued from above was left on the shop floor to a labour force which was then divided up to perform a great number of detailed tasks. Although the basic skills required by a detail worker were greatly underestimated by Taylor — the "Ox" from Bohemia whom he describes and derides was in fact a man who had built his own house — nevertheless the workers were alienated from the work they did, both by their loss of control over the whole production process and by their ignorance of the value which their detailed work added to the product. While they hung on to their

differential skills as long as they could, it was a losing battle. But their shared sense of deprivation and exploitation gave them a unity and strength in united action which was always a threat to the owners of capital. All this has changed. In the advanced industrial countries workers have for long been offered a high wage for their alienated work, and now the machines are being transformed.

The new technology incorporates a whole range of automated and semi- automated technical systems which have displaced many of the skills of manual workers and even of non-manual workers. If the first Industrial Revolution replaced the muscles of legs and backs and arms of men with mechanical power and greatly speeded up their movements, the latest Industrial Revolution is replacing human brain power and enormously speeding up its calculations and long distance communication. Indeed, the processing of information is at the heart of the new technology and has more than anything else generated the new ways of organising work and of structuring economic activities. On the one hand, the new information systems have enabled the span of control to be much widened. Many widely separated units of production and distribution can now be controlled from one centre; and thus the size of companies and the concentration of capital has been greatly increased. Take-overs and mergers have abounded until a few hundred transnational companies exercise control world-wide over the greater part of all productive industry and commerce. On the other hand, the introduction of flexible automation into machine processes has made possible the decentralisation of production to quite small units scattered all over the world. There still have to be a number of large-scale assembly points in the case of motor cars and other vehicles; but for many products assembly can take place almost anywhere near to a large market, with components fed in from widespread suppliers making use of large scale bulk transport by sea or road or rail or even by air. Huge savings are made as a result of ending the need to hold stocks, since point of sale recording and ordering enables the required product to be delivered "just in time", where once it had to be held "just in case", and might prove not to be what was wanted.

It is this new technology that lies behind the changes in the structure and location of employment which we have noticed. At first sight, these changes appeared greatly to weaken the application of workers' power. Can they be turned to the advantage of workers? There are some who see in flexible automation a potential end to the alienation of workers and the opening up of a new opportunity for that free association of workers, which Marx and Engels envisaged — a commonwealth of co-operative self-managed production units linked together by exchange agreements within a general allocation of resources made by congresses representative of the workers councils from all the many units. This model has been most powerfully restated in recent years by Ernest Mandel in reply to his critics who confused the bureaucratically fashioned plan of the Soviet type command economy with the democratic planning by self-managing workers' councils and their joint congresses.

Mandel distanced himself from the 1980s Gorbachev model of self-managed enterprises for the Soviet Union, operating within a framework of centrally determined norms, such as was advanced by his one-time economic adviser, Abel Aganbegyan. Mandel saw this as conceding far too much to the market — Gorbachev's policies were to move still further towards the market model after 1989 — and retaining too much bureaucratic power in the hands of the ministries at the centre, without any real political control coming by means of a revolution from below. But Mandel's associated workers' councils making policy through thirty or forty sectoral congresses to one supreme resource allocating body, is not beyond criticism from the viewpoint of one seeking to ensure democratic control. Mandel's assumption that most needs can be met by the simple replication of standing orders runs quite contrary to the modern desire for change and variety. There is a fundamental difficulty for Mandel in trying to accommodate such expressions of consumer choice in a model which bestows all the power upon organisations of producers.

This was at the heart of the criticism made of the Marx-Mandel model in an important recent article by Diane Elson. "It prioritises power," she wrote, "to those who produce the goods and services and ignores the needs of people using the goods and services in producing and reproducing labour power." She was not only making the point that the first will probably be mainly men and the second mainly women, but that emphasis on the interests of workers at the point of production will tend to overlay the interests of workers and their families as consumers. This emphasis has been the persistent cause of consumers' complaints coming from the Soviet Union and Eastern Europe and has been in large part the background to the revolt against communist governments in those countries. In fact the new technology with its flexible capacity to adapt to innovation has hardly reached these countries, except in the military sector. So we could not expect to see it put to use to bring producers and consumers together in quite new ways, but it was certainly Aganbegyan's belief that the new technology could be used to combine more self- management by producers with greater involvement of consumers in the democratic planning of resource allocation.

Since the new technology has been introduced by the giant transnational companies of the capitalist world, no one should be surprised to find that it has been designed to channel profits more effectively into these centres of capital accumulation. That is nothing new in capitalism, but there are two new implications in its introduction which are of relevance for the creation of openings for the advance of workers' power. The first is that the pace of technological change and innovation has become so fast and the scale of any single company's operations so vast that a degree of mutual co-operation as well as of competition has had to be established by the several governments which have the operations of such companies within their sphere of responsibility. This co-operation under the aegis of government does not consist as of old merely in state finance and state protection of national companies, but of state involvement in the actual decisions on product choice and design. Such government intervention and partnership has been most notable in the case of Japan through the Ministry of International Trade and Industry (MITI), but not much less in the USA through the War Department, and increasingly through the European Commission in the European Community. If government involvement is required to this degree in company management, democratic accountability for such involvement has to enter the political agenda. The failure of British governments over the years to go beyond macro-economic management of home demand and the overseas balance of payments, and to dirty their hands with the actual business of production and commerce, derives from a class divided education system and one that esteems literacy over numeracy and the pure sciences over technology. It has been fatal for British industrial competition with Japan, West Germany and the USA. A more educated work force in Britain from top to bottom, comparable with that of its competitors, could begin to reduce Britain's democratic deficit as well as its foreign payments deficit. The further failure of British governments to recognise the potential in the European Community for restructuring European industry to face Japanese and United States competition has been equally unfortunate not only for British competitiveness but from the point of view of exercising some democratic control over the unaccountable power of the great companies. The absolute failure of the trade unions especially in the UK to come to terms with the new technology on an international scale will be taken up later in this chapter.

The second implication of the new technology for the extension of popular power is to be seen in the fact that the great retail companies have been taking the lead in its application and particularly in their use of the new communication systems. Their whole aim has been to discover and to shape the public's needs and to supply them — or at least those members of the public who are better off — with a great variety of products to meet consumer choice. The power of the (moneyed) consumer has been greatly enhanced, and with this has come a much increased awareness of consumer power. Before the introduction of the new technology, the mass marketing of standardised products coming from giant plants with production lines geared to long runs had its implications for government demand management, for standardised education and welfare provision, for mass unions and centralised bargaining and for two party political systems around class divisions in society. These are the social relations associated together in what has come to be described as "Fordism". By the same token "Post-Fordism", which follows from the new technology, implies not only more decentralised government intervention in the networks of production and distribution around autonomous profit centres in more diversified markets, but a more differentiated education and health service, localised trade union bargaining, and multi-party systems built upon a plurality of social movements.

Consumer unions

If this is accepted as a valid distinction, then it follows that the agences of social change must be more diverse, more pluralistic, more localised, more nuanced than the classic concept of the massed armies of a homogeneous working class battering down the walls of privilege and power. The many niches in capitalist societies which those with special skills and accomplishments have been able to create for themselves and occupy — in sport, in the popular arts and in the media and advertising — have to be recognised. Most important of all, the role of women and the demands of women have to be elevated, and understood as something different as well as equally justified as those of men. The plurality of special interest groups and popular organisations concerned with advancing particular causes — in recreation, education, health, child care, housing, civil liberties, concern for the elderly, conservation and environmental protection, whole food, fair trade, etc. — indicates an opening up of political activity into wider fields than the traditional arenas of the economy, defence and law and order. This is the real basis for Diane Elson's counterposing of consumer unions to the hegemony of workers' councils in Mandel's Marxist model.

Linking together all these separate interests into one synergy suggests the method of networking in place of the hierarchies of economic organisation or the monoliths of political party structures.

The consumers' union is presented as a mobilising body, not only monitoring and advising on the quality and safety of goods and services, but researching and advocating new forms of provision and even placing pilot orders with producer organisations on behalf of consumers. Local, regional and national networks would be established between producer and consumer groups for information exchange and for the organisation of political influence. These would respect the independence of each other and would not be based on hierarchies of power or flows of capital accumulation. Looking forward to a radical shift in the structures of political and economic power, Diane Elson envisages popularly accountable state regulating bodies licensing public enterprise and setting wage norms, prices and investment targets for self-managing groups of workers in production and distribution. Basic social services, health and education and other public services would be free and subject to popular control, but overall resource allocation and economic management would be under central authority, subject to the influence equally of producer and consumer unions. This is her answer to Mandel's congresses of workers' councils.

There is very much to be said for this networking system in linking producers and consumers, as we have noted in earlier chapters, where relations between First and Third World organisations were being considered. Networks of consumer and producer groups inside the First World could become a prototype, even within a capitalist framework, for an alternative to both the wartime and Soviet type command economy and to the minimally regulated market system. To explore the ways in which networks could operate as a challenge to the power over the market of the giant companies we have to invent a framework which ensures

a) strong regulation of network operations that provides for resource allocation to correct inequalities and environmental damage without a oppressive centralised command structure;
b) freedom for producer and consumer unions to manage their own investment and pricing policies in competition with each other without the anarchy of unplanned markets.

The central requirement is that the framework should be one that recognises organised groups or unions, whether of producers or consumers or activists in other social relations. Mrs Thatcher's extraordinary conclusion that there was no such thing as society,

but only individuals and families, may have been wishful thinking
— that she wanted no intermediaries between Her Mistress's voice
and the family sitting round the TV set at home. It totally overlooked
the undeniable fact that in Britain at least, and almost certainly
elsewhere in Europe and North America, the overwhelming majority
of the adult population belongs to some club or voluntary
association as well as a trade union, and that most belong to more
than one. It is this desire to participate that networks can serve to
bring together and mobilise for common objectives. Diane Elson
envisages each consumer household as a member of a national
consumer union, which would have networking relations with
producer organisations. But the very idea of a union of consumer
households is really quite inadequate as a vehicle for the kind of
participation which we are looking for to replace either the passive
acceptance of commands or isolated activity in the market. It denies,
moreover, the main object of networking, unless the households
have first formed themselves into some kind of grouping, some on
a local basis, some on the basis of special interests.

It is their horizontal linkages which we originally emphasised as
the essence of networks. A vast union of individual households,
stores and factories on the scale of Marks and Spencer does not
sound like a network, and Marks at least has competition from other
big retailers. A pluralist society should have as many unions and
associations as people have interests, on the same principle as there
were to be guilds in the concept of Guild Socialism proposed by
GDH Cole and other syndicalists during and after the First World
War. It can be argued that the new technology and especially the
new information systems have made these early socialist ideas
much more realisable.

Some people fear that competition would continue to be both
wasteful and divisive. But monopolies are very much less to be
desired. I can rely on the good will of one milk roundsman and one
paper shop and just one supplier of several other such services in
my village, because of the pressure of local opinion, but I would
not wish to depend on one source for all my groceries or other
consumer goods. Diane Elson puts her faith in limitations placed
upon any positional competition, which implies exclusivity in deals.
But all competition is to some extent positional — if my consumer
union has contacts with a particular producer, others are excluded.
Diane Elson believes that fair competition "could be reinforced by
the development of a professional code of behaviour for the staff
of consumer unions, such as regulates the activities of groups like
doctors, lawyers and architects in Western European countries."
There is in fact some quite fierce competition in these professions

and the only reason it is not positional is that the professional bodies exercise some control over entry, so that there is work, if not the most lucrative work, for all. In every market economy competition is regulated, as we have seen, both by common law and by legislation on health and safety standards, fair trade descriptions, minimum wages, and so on. The main point is that it is surely a mistake to try to set limits to the number of competing consumer unions. A natural limit would be set for any individual household by the simple fact that subscription to each would not be without cost.

What would really make a difference to the accountability of the consumer-producer networks that we are considering, both to their internal democracy and their external power, would be that they should be firmly based on local communities. These might in some cases be ethnic communities, as was earlier suggested, or possibly communities of taste — whole food enthusiasts, vegetarians, francophiles, etc. More often, one would hope and expect, the basis would be a shared locality, housing estate, block of flats, village or street, where groups were formed which began to forge links as consumers with local producers, so that the division into consumers and producers, which the market creates inside all of us, could be healed at its base. Diane Elson's model included some local unions for local services, but after that, economies of scale, she thought, demanded that we should all belong to very large unions which would be distinguished only by the range of goods they supply. In capitalist market economies the supermarkets started by specialising to some extent, but increasingly in their new drive-in stores they aim to supply almost everything on the one vast site, as do Harrods or Selfridges in London. The crucial point for the consumer is that there is more than one to choose from, but sales are directed towards the relatively affluent. Would it be possible for networks to compete with these giants, by working on a smaller and more localised scale, and still meet the needs of the less affluent? The history of the co-operative retail businesses which tried to do this is not encouraging. Is there no alternative?

Popular networks at different levels

One alternative would be to break down the goods and services we all need into several different levels of provision — local, regional , national, international — and to encourage networks at these several levels to develop on a self-financing basis. This is what I proposed in the last chapter of my book on *Models in Political Economy*. The weakness of that schema was somewhat similar to the weakness in Diane Elson's model. My networks had width at each level, but no clear vertical linkages, except for money grants from above. The upward influence was missing. Her networks have depth into national and international production facilities, but no clear horizontal linkages. What would the model look like if we tried to combine the two, connecting consumer groups and producing enterprises at each level and dipping into the national and international pool of resources when needed?

Let us first recall the reasons for challenging the current workings of a market economy. First, it fails to meet the needs of the poorer consumers — the best bargains are in the drive-in stores, which are out of their reach ; second, it fails to control waste of resources and damage to the environment resulting from cost cutting practices; third, such cost cutting competition leads also to exploitation of labour world-wide. How would an alternative work on the basis of networking? It is clear that it would be impossible to establish such a whole new system all at once, except after some cataclysmic phenomenon like a war or a great slump, which is not something to be desired. Nonetheless, if parts of the system were to be put in place and operated successfully as prototypes of new economic relations, confidence would be created in the possibility of developing the whole.

If we start from the bottom with the housing estate, village or block of flats, having perhaps a thousand households, they can be envisaged forming groups to elect community councils. These would then have responsibilities for certain services — cleaning, laundering, gardening, plumbing, electrical faults and minor building repairs — for which they could make a charge, and also for renting out premises for workshops and retail outlets, shops, restaurants etc. from which they would get an income to use for their own purposes, improving their environment, recreation grounds, parks, creches, etc. Through horizontal linkages they would network with similar estates and villages or blocks of flats in wards and districts including the surrounding countryside, both to provide appropriate services at that level in housing, health, education, rubbish collection, foot paths, swimming pools, larger parks and playing fields, and to draw upon those enterprises producing mainly for local needs — fruit and vegetables and other local foods, bakeries, housing materials, repair shops etc. Contracts and prices would then be the subject of negotiation on quality and service between representatives of the workers, the groups of households and the local authority at this district level. These authorities would, of course, need also to obtain supplies for their activities from outside their district. This could be done by building links with particular enterprises, whose products suited their needs.

By adding here the element of networking, these links could be strengthened into a strong and continuing relationship, allowing for forward planning beyond a single purchase or contract. This happens now, where public purchasing officers have found a supplier they can rely on, who understands their special needs. District authorities could also help to finance specialised networks of groups of people, such as ethnic minorities, who wanted to develop provision for their own particular needs and tastes.

In this model, the communities and districts form the real building blocks of decentralised power, with their own elected councils and much extended responsibilities. For it is at this level that people can meet each other and get to know each other's interests, share common facilities, and feel a common responsibility for the care and protection of the neighbourhood. This scheme is designed for extending social provision. But of course, people still have personal needs and household needs, and many of these can only be met efficiently, as Diane Elson insists, on the very large scale of ·the supermarket chains. Local community considerations become of much less importance in organising an alternative for household provision to the dominance of a few big suppliers. The criticism which we made earlier of the big companies was that it was profitable for them to cater primarily for the better-off customer. The hypermarket stores reveal this very clearly. There is no doubt about their capacity for innovation, and the efficiency of their systems of procurement and quality control, but the tendency to establish stores on out of town sites means that only customers with cars can make use of them; and in Britain nearly 40% of households have no access to a motor car. How could personal and household requirements be met in ways that do not exclude such a large proportion of the population?

There are two ways of tackling such inequalities in provision. The first is to ensure a more equal distribution of incomes by taxation and incomes policies. The second is to strengthen the voting power of the poorer members of the community. The 40% of households without cars are a minority, and can be outvoted by the majority. Quite apart from the fact that it may become necessary to reduce the number of private cars on the roads and encourage the use of public transport, there is a strong case in any democratic society for giving support to minorities. In the market, as we noticed, the pull of money operates, and not the pull of people. If people's power (the real meaning of democracy) is to be strengthened, it must be by public support. Our district and community councils can do much to strengthen social provision for all. But in the provision of personal and household needs, we shall have to bring a higher level of power to bear, where large companies can be deployed to make up for individual financial weakness. Cities and counties comprise populations of several millions, and it is to them that we should look for the necessary power to influence household provision, so that the needs of the poorer households are catered for.

At the level of the city and county, we are not only dealing with a much larger population, and the services of health, education, police, fire brigades, and public transport appropriate to that scale, but there will be productive enterprises sited within their territories — factories, mines and quarries, refineries and the like which inevitably have a national, as well as an international, market. It would be reasonable to imagine loosely vertically integrated competing networks being based on cities and counties.

In this case, the power of a city or county authority would be enough to ensure that suppliers inside the network catered for the full range of income groups equally. Regional differences in incomes and in tastes could then be allowed for: something that several of the supermarket chains are already beginning to recognise. If cities and counties build up their own network of suppliers, there is no reason why they should not link up with other neighbouring cities and counties to widen their network of households, communities and supplying enterprises. The scale of the network can be pushed just as far as is necessary for efficiency in a competition that need not be positional, because there is likely to be room for a quite large number of networks in a country the size of Great Britain, for example.

There remains the question of the relationship of the producing enterprises to the networks and to the central planning departments of state and federation. Some of the enterprises may be quite large, supplying several, or even many, networks. They will want to have direct relations with the state and federal power, since both will have the capacity to set norms for their operations, and to see that they are observed. The anarchy of the over-decentralised economic structure in Yugoslavia stands as an awful warning of what happens if this central power is abandoned.

In Diane Elson's model, however, the individual enterprises are not to be self-financing; although they would be subject to cross-subsidisation, and therefore presumably to general trading policy direction by the network consumer union. By withholding both the power to set prices and the power to make investment decisions from the enterprises as well as from the networks, not only is the central state and federal power enormously augmented, but no means of self-discipline is left to the enterprises. Efficiency is to be rewarded and inefficiency penalised by the network managers' instructions, responding to their members interests. But how is efficiency to be measured? We discussed this earlier, in relation to Soviet central planning and the decision to decentralise under the new economic *perestroika* to self-managing, and self-financing, enterprises operating within the parameters of centrally determined "normatives". Negotiation between the networks and the enterprises, about the actual requirements of consumers, provides the networking element that replaces market forces; but the lesson of our earlier discussion is that both would then have to be free to manage themselves, and finance themselves, within the parameters set by central government.

Given the great plurality of networks which is envisaged here, rather than the few all-powerful ministries in a command economy, or even the presumably quite limited number of vertically integrated competing blocks in Diane Elson's model, effective representation of these networks at the centre has to be provided for. The setting of parameters for the operation of both networks and enterprises seems likely to imply something more continuous than occasional rounds of negotiation. One solution to this problem would be an economic Parliament based on the networks; a second chamber, to complement the political chamber based on geographical constituencies. This would need to be replicated at a federal as well as nation state level. These chambers would have a preparatory function, reviewing performance in a way that select committees of the British House of Commons do now, but going much further than they do in proposing new measures in advance of government action. This would go far to reduce the increasingly unaccountable power of civil servants and commissioners and government ministers, and especially of Prime Ministers and their closest advisers, to do as they will. How the networks were represented would be a matter for discussion, but some reserved places should be ensured, not only for the representatives of the hundreds of thousands of communities, and the several thousand urban and rural districts, but also of the several hundred independent networks representing minorities, not only ethnic, but large groups, like pensioners and the disabled, and whole food and vegetarian believers.

It seems best to sum up the proposals made in this section in a direct and personal way. I live in a village where the Parish meeting elects parish councillors, and I vote regularly for (generally against!) a district councillor, as well as a county councillor to represent me in local affairs, and an MP in the national Parliament, and now also an MEP in the European Parliament. When we have a system of economic networks and economic Parliaments I shall vote for them too. I shall decide, with my household, what activities to join. I assume that there will be two or three local networks; one based on my village, one on several local villages in our district, and one each on the two nearest towns. One of these is a city, and both the city and our county will have networks linked to major producing enterprises and supermarket outlets. There will also be one or more specialist networks (that I may indeed have helped to create) linked to whole food products, Third World solidarity organisations, workers co-operatives and so on. There is nothing to stop us joining them all, although there may be some initial subscription or registration fee to pay that checks my pluralistic enthusiasm. As I am also employed in the locality I shall join a local trade union, and influence union and enterprise policy, and when I am a pensioner, the local branch of the OAP association.

As a member of each of these networks I can vote for, and stand for, membership of a Network Council at village, district, county and national level, and for the whole food, solidarity and workers' co-operative networks, and for my trade union at various levels. In all of these ways I shall expect to exercise an influence, with my family, and my village, and my fellow workers, on the political decisions about priorities at various levels, but also on the economic decisions about the quality and range of goods and services available, and the source of their supply. I shall expect further, that the various networks which I support will have their say in the Economic Parliaments, and that this will have its effect on the decisions of the central and federal government. Of course, I may remain in a minority on many issues, but I have a wide choice of alternative sources for the goods and services that my family needs, and, through the specialised networks that I belong to, I will know that our special interests are represented, and that community as well as private provision receives its full acknowledgement in national planning of resource allocation. I will also be able to see that workers' co-operatives have a role to play alongside other small private enterprises, in addition to the many, much larger, publicly and privately owned enterprises, in supplying the various networks. I shall, moreover, have an interest in the international links of the networks to which I and my family belong, and which have been described in earlier chapters.

A conclusion on networks and national co-ordination

This is not the place to describe the overall economic structure built around economic networks, which might replace the present national economic structures and the present international economic order, dominated by superpowers and giant transnational companies. Nor can we indicate here the nature of the transformation from one to the other. One can hardly imagine the change involving less than a long drawn out and bitter struggle to replace the power of the few by the power of the many. The struggle for an economic democracy to complement the struggle for political democracy has hardly begun. Both struggles have been severely hampered by the absence of either economic or political democracy in those countries where social ownership has been introduced in place of private capital. They have been still further weakened by the absence of an alternative economic and political model to those built either around the market or around central planning, both of which are now seriously discredited.

The exploration of the role of networks is designed to discover their potential as a prototype building block of a new order, which could perhaps be developed as an embryo of a new birth in the womb of the old society. We have seen that networks can offer a third way between the blind market and the totalitarian all-seeing plan, that does more than give eyes to the market and democratise the plan. The essential difference can be seen in the key role of the networker, and the contrast of this role with either the salesmen, advertisers, brokers, financiers and the speculators in the market on the one hand, or the hierarchy of bureaucrats and their nominees in the command economy. Whether it would be possible for the same men and women to change roles would depend on a whole sea-change in the ethos of society from a casino of competitive speculators on one side and militarised cohorts of Myrmidons on the other. Networkers are not necessarily individuals but may be companies, co-operatives or associations working for fees or commissions. They will be especially necessary as wholesalers, merchants and shippers who play such a central role in markets. It is the absolute absence of such intermediaries between ministries and enterprises in the Soviet economy that has made its transfer from commands to markets so difficult.

It is not at all the idea that there would be no place for the skills of the entrepreneur, seizing on new ideas, putting them together in workable packages, bringing men and women together to combine their manifold capacities in co-operative endeavour, nor for the skills of the administrator in drawing up plans and constructing systems for monitoring and reviewing progress, and making and adjusting working procedures. But these skills would be made to serve not just the individual private company and transnational corporation, or the amorphous department of state, but actual people in living and working communities, determining their own needs, contributing their own understanding to the making of a genuine commonwealth. Many entrepreneurs in market economies and administrators in planned economies may well believe, or wish, that they were serving the people by their efforts. They may indeed well be doing so, but they are not involving people. It is the whole purpose of networks to involve more and more people in determining their own lives, not just as individuals, as households or even as narrow communities, but as wider and wider communities, with a multiplicity of interlocking interests and purposes.

It is not at all the idea, either, that there would be no place for money in a networking economy. Some exchanges might take place by barter, but monetary measures and monetary accounting would still be needed as a generalised control over the use of resources. Measures of energy consumption, to support a carbon tax, for example, and measures of the use of other scarce resources, together with measures of past and present labour inputs, will be needed to supplement overall monetary measures. Some societies might well move to providing a wider range of goods and services on free supply, but a world of abundance, in which we all draw from a common pool according to our needs, is still very far in the future. The purpose of networks is to make the links between people as producers and people as consumers more direct, and to emphasise our common social needs, as much as our individual personal needs, in this way to make for less inequalities in the enjoyment of resources and less profligacy in their use.

The financing of networks and of their associated enterprises has been a key issue in the distinction I have wished to draw between Diane Elson's consumer union led networks, and my community based networks. We almost certainly agree in emphasising community needs rather than household needs. But, the rejection by Diane Elson of a monetary motivation through the ability to set prices in the case of both networks and enterprises, is a major point of difference. Her enterprises are not expected to be self-financing, and her networks are not expected to be getting their income from sales, but rather from their grants and capitation fees. In my model, both networks and enterprises have to pay their way from income they earn directly, or on commission, from sales of goods and services. Any network or enterprise that fails will have to be reconstructed by the authority that founded it. In the case of large national networks or enterprises, a central state or federal body will have to be brought into the restructuring process. Where networks and enterprises succeed, they will accumulate funds, and, within general parameters set by government, they should be free to use these as they wish, but the networking principle will mean that this is a matter for negotiation between representatives of the networking groups, the founding local authority and the enterprise workers. None of this, however, can replace the ultimate co-ordinative function of central nation state or federal government, although the communities, the networks and the enterprises, should all be involved in the preparation and negotiation of central plans, whether through Economic Parliaments or through other means.

Economic co-ordination by central government has been almost total in the depth and width of its embrace in centrally planned economies, but it should not be thought to be absent in capitalist market economies. Under a so-called liberalising regime such as that of the Thatcher government in Britain, it appears that most of the economic co-ordination was left to market forces; but in effect, the power of the state was used overwhelmingly to limit the powers of all other countervailing forces in the market which could act against the power of the giant transnational companies; it has especially sought to reduce the power of trade unions and local authorities, and despite the rhetoric, of small businesses also. The reduction of levels of taxation may well have increased the freedom of the rich; it certainly reduced the freedom of the poor. Public power at state or federal level is needed to redistribute resources between public and private spending, and between higher and lower income brackets, to ensure conservation of resources and protection of the environment, and to provide an element of co-ordination.

The main areas where co-ordination is required are the following: first, the allocation of resources between regions so as to correct any long-term backwardness or threat of impoverishment from changing industrial structures; second, the redistribution of income and wealth to correct major inequalities and to protect those who are dependent on social income, such as pensioners, the disabled, the unemployed; third, the allocation of resources between different sectors according to popular demand, but taking into account the conservation of resources, protection of the environment, international competitive position etc.; fourth, setting the balance between consumption and investment overall in the light of long-term development requirements; fifth, ensuring the external balance of the movement of goods and services and capital, where we have seen that imbalances are a chronic cause of less than optimum growth world-wide; sixth, the setting of prices for basic materials and of price norms to control monopoly pricing and regulate general inflation.

While I have allowed more freedom to the networks and enterprises in the setting of prices and investment decisions in the model here outlined, I am not unmindful of the need for strong central control at federal and state levels to prevent decentralisation descending into anarchy. I would justify this preference for generosity by the continuing competitive power of the various enterprises and networks, by the democratic accountability of the networks, by the absence of an overwhelming requirement for survival that any of them should achieve dominating power. I am, in effect, more frightened of excessive power in the hands of governments than I am of any excess of power among the networks. In the long run, the power of the nation states and federations of states, and particularly of the super powers, will have to be brought within the framework of a new international economic order. The prospect of world government is far distant, and it would be no advance on the present world disorder if it implied a world-wide command economy. The proposals we have considered for international networking and long term agreements between nations on trade exchanges and technology transfer, suggest what might be building blocks for a new economic order. But the networking process would inevitably be limited until some of the original ideas of John Maynard Keynes for a World Bank, Monetary Fund, World Money and International Trade Organisation can be revived, after all the distortion that they have suffered at the hands of a hegemonic United States of America.

Despite the massive show of force in the Gulf War, even because of it, that era of United States hegemony could soon be over. We shall have the chance to think again about Europe's relationship with the developing nations which were all once its colonies and about the directions of change which a new technology makes possible for everyone in increasingly pluralistic societies. Peace and security in the Middle East and throughout the world will only be possible if inequalities of wealth are greatly reduced and if new and genuinely inter-national institutions are created, through which peoples, and not only states, can make their voices heard. When the killing stops, there will perhaps be just one last chance for Europeans to show that they can help to rebuild the lives of Third World peoples that for three hundred years they have in effect been destroying.

References

Michael H. Best, *The New Competition: Institutions of Industrial Restructuring*, Polity Press, 1990

André Gorz, *Farewell to the Working Class*, Pluto Press, 1980

Ken Coates & Tony Topham, *Industrial Democracy in Great Britain*, MacGibbon & Key, 1968, chapters 2 and 3.

Central Statistical Office, *Social Trends 19*, HM Stationery Office, London, 1989

Robin Murray, "Ownership, Control and the Market", *New Left Review*, No.164, July-August 1987.

Abel Aganbegyan, *The Challenge: Economics of Perestroika*, Hutchinson, 1988.

Ernest Mandel, "In Defence of Socialist Planning", *New Left Review*, No.159, Sept.-Oct., 1986. "The Myth of Market Socialism", *New Left Review*, No.169, May-June 1988.

Diane Elson, "Market Socialism or Socialisation of the Market", *New Left Review*, No.172, Nov.-Dec., 1988.

Michael Barratt Brown, *Models in Political Economy*, Penguin, 1984

SOCIALIST GROUP
EUROPEAN PARLIAMENT

European Labour Forum

Socialism through the back door.

Come in!
Don't bother to knock!

Elf is a journal of politics edited by Ken Coates MEP.

Subscription details are available from:

Bertrand Russell House
Gamble Street
Nottingham
NG7 4ET
England

Telephone (0)602 708318
Fax (0)602 420433